Vivid praise for Laurie Sandell's

THE
IMPOSTOR'S DAUGHTER
A True Memoir

"An eloquent graphic memoir." —Lev Grossman, *Time*

"*The Impostor's Daughter* is the mesmerizing account of Laurie Sandell's hunt for the truth about her father. Maybe he's a con man, possibly he's delusional, but to Laurie he's a larger-than-life figure— the most adventurous father in the world. Compellingly told and wonderfully drawn, *The Impostor's Daughter* is also the story of Laurie's personal struggle with pop-culture's zeitgeist trifecta: sex, celebrity, and substance abuse. It's a stirring debut."
— Nathan Englander, author of *The Ministry of Special Cases* and *For the Relief of Unbearable Urges*

"Sophisticated and spellbinding, Laurie Sandell's graphic memoir is rife with dramatic family dynamics, secrets, and subterfuges centered around her mysterious, mercurial Argentine American father. By uncovering the buried truths of his past life, she claims her own coming-of-age story." —*Elle*

"Don't pick up *The Impostor's Daughter* if you have an urgent looming deadline. You'll start reading and then keep reading till you reach the last page, because this real-life detective story is so compelling, personal, and poignant that you'll end up ignoring your own life and responsibilities. Like I did."
—A. J. Jacobs, author of *The Know-It-All* and *The Year of Living Biblically*

"Sandell melds solid writing chops with solid artwork to produce a terrific graphic memoir. . . . The truth shakes up her world, which was pretty shaky anyway. In Sandell's skilled hands, all that shakiness makes for a terrific read."

—Martin Zimmerman, *San Diego Union-Tribune*

"A stunner. From the opening page, I was hooked. This coming-of-age tale for grown-ups may be a feast for the eyes, but it's also a sock in the gut—a wrenchingly funny tale of deception, addiction, and what it means to search for true love when you were raised on lies. You'll finish this page-turner in a single night—but the story will stay with you for much longer."

—Carole Radziwill, author of *What Remains*

"Sandell's gifts for constructing a compelling narrative with highly emotional building blocks, providing perspective and shading (literally) with engaging and expressive images, and baring her own weaknesses make *The Impostor's Daughter* insightful and dramatic. . . . Consider this a great crossover candidate for admirers of memoirs like Jeannette Walls's *The Glass Castle*."

—Francisca Goldsmith, *Booklist*

"An absorbing graphic memoir. . . . This smart, candid book with its vivid illustrations is a must-read."   —*InStyle*

"Like Alison Bechdel's *Fun Home,* Sandell lays out the details of her story so completely that it's hard not to turn the page. Along the way, she also talks about her personal relationships, struggles with substance abuse, and random e-mails with Ashley Judd. Why you'll like it: Because you love *Gilmore Girls* and women's magazines and you've never read a graphic novel, but you really keep meaning to start. Because your father is kind of crazy, too. Because, quite simply, you have a couple free hours on Sunday and you need a great read."   —*USA Today*

"Sandell's wit shines through her clever illustrations and honest prose."   —Korina Lopez, *USA Today*

"Delightfully composed. . . . A touchingly youthful story about a daughter's gushing love for her father. Using a winning mixture of straightforward comic-book illustrations with a first-person diary-like commentary, Sandell recounts the gradual realization from her young adulthood onward that her charming, larger-than-life Argentine father, bragging of war medals, degrees from prestigious universities, and acquaintances with famous people, had lied egregiously to his family about his past and accomplishments. . . . Sandell's method of storytelling is marvelously unique and will surely spark imitators."

—*Publishers Weekly*

"Sandell's unique story, told in comic-strip-style drawings, is part mystery, part coming-of-age tale—and a thoroughly provocative read."

—*Redbook*

"With its intense family drama, rogues' gallery of boyfriends, and celebrity interviews, *The Impostor's Daughter* will make Laurie Sandell's regular readers at *Glamour* very happy. But this instantly likable, brightly illustrated graphic memoir will also earn her fans who never pick up a glossy magazine. . . . Like Alison Bechdel's masterful graphic memoir *Fun Home,* this book tackles family dysfunction, driven by a daughter's investigation of her father's dirty secrets. Each does a great job of rendering in deft visual shorthand the emotional stew of denial, guilt, and anger. . . . Sandell is understandably conflicted about revealing her father's past. But the truth has a way of emerging—although never with such wonderful four-color illustrations."

—Karen Schechner, *Cleveland Plain Dealer*

"*The Impostor's Daughter* is funny, frank, and absolutely engaging. It's about truth and consequences and families and men and women and fame and, well, life itself. It's wonderful."

—Susan Orlean, author of *The Orchid Thief*

"Much of Laurie Sandell's story—addiction, conflicted family loyalty, uncertain love, a damaging father—has been told before. So then why is her *The Impostor's Daughter* the best book I've read in ages?

Maybe it's because, in the style of the even-more-personal *Persepolis,* Sandell chose to tell her story in graphic form. Her vibrantly colored drawings are simple, but expressive—and often funny. . . . It makes perfect sense that Sandell's story, in which she rails against the outrageous web of lies that her father has constructed, would hide nothing. . . . The visual nature of the book makes this possible: Sandell lays her life (and her father's life) bare—allowing for a strikingly honest, intimate self-portrait. . . . In the end, though, what makes Sandell's memoir so enthralling is how very ordinary much of the story is. Very few have a deceitful con artist for a father, but surely everyone has gone through periods of wondering what to do with their lives. . . . The way that Sandell blends the totally off-the-wall with the universally familiar is what finally raises *The Impostor's Daughter* above other memoirs. And by the time you're finished reading it, which I promise will be soon after you start, you'll be reluctantly thankful for Sandell's father's misdeeds—without them, his daughter would never have created this truly wonderful work of art."

—Elizabeth Simins, *Buffalo News*

THE
IMPOSTOR'S DAUGHTER

A TRUE MEMOIR

LAURIE SANDELL

BACK BAY BOOKS
Little, Brown and Company
New York Boston London

For all the
truth tellers

Back Bay Books / Little, Brown and Company
Hachette Book Group
237 Park Avenue, New York, NY 10017
www.hachettebookgroup.com

Originally published in hardcover by Little, Brown and Company,
July 2009
First Back Bay paperback edition, July 2010

Back Bay Books is an imprint of Little, Brown and Company.
The Back Bay Books name and logo are trademarks of Hachette
Book Group, Inc.

Author's Note: Some people's names were changed to respect
and protect their identities. Bill, Ben, Elsa, Jimmy B., Giulia
Russo, Gustavo Torres, Marcus Kipplinger, Walter Matheson,
Mai Feng, and the names of the clients at the Shades of Hope
are all pseudonyms.

Color by Paige Pooler

Library of Congress Cataloging-in-Publication Data
Sandell, Laurie.
  The impostor's daughter : a true memoir / Laurie Sandell
    p. cm.
  ISBN 978-0-316-03305-3 (hc) / 978-0-316-03306-0 (pb)
1. Sandell, Laurie—Comic books, strips, etc. 2. Journalists—
United States—Biography—Comic books, strips, etc. 3. Graphic
novels. I. Title.
  PN4874.S2687A3 2009
  070.92—dc22   2008034091
[B]

10 9 8 7 6 5 4 3 2 1

Printed in China

READING GROUP GUIDE

THE
IMPOSTOR'S DAUGHTER

A ᵀᴿᵁᴱ MEMOIR

BY LAURIE SANDELL

Laurie Sandell talks with Merrill Markoe about the origins of *The Impostor's Daughter*

Merrill Markoe is an Emmy Award–winning television writer; a cocreator of The Late Show with David Letterman; *an author of eight novels, including the bestselling* Walking in Circles Before Lying Down *and* Nose Up, Eyes Down; *and a lay expert on narcissism. She and Laurie Sandell met when Sandell edited a piece Markoe wrote for* Glamour *about the women of* Saturday Night Live.

MERRILL MARKOE: When I first met you, I wrote a piece for *Glamour,* and you were my editor, and you were pretty much invisible at first. Then you sent me that piece you wrote for *Esquire* about your dad. And suddenly you were this other person, and you and I became friends. It struck me that your dad's identity provided a second level of service for you, just as it had for him.

LAURIE SANDELL: I always knew the power of that story. For years I thought it was the most compelling thing about me, so it was the first thing I offered up to people I admired. In a way, you could say this book is another offshoot of that.

MM: But this book is really about you processing the whole thing. You were thrown into this without any permission asked, so you made lemonade out of lemons.

LS: It's true. I was taking ownership of my personal story, after being raised on all these lies. I was saying, you might have an idea of how you'd like to present your story, but I have a right to tell my story, too.

MM: That's a hard thing to do with the guy still alive. Right now I'm writing a piece about crazy mothers for a book of essays I'm doing, and I have nothing but friends with crazy mothers. But most of them don't want their names used, so I call them Anonymous Friend number 1, Anonymous Friend number 2 . . .

LS: Well, it took me a long time to feel comfortable exposing my father. As you know, I wrote the *Esquire* piece anonymously.

MM: You were interviewing him for two years for that story, on tape. And he was cooperating.

LS: Yes. When we started, I knew my father had amazing stories; I knew he was eccentric; I knew he led an unknowable, mysterious life. I even suspected he might be in the CIA. But I had no idea I was going to write a piece called "My Father, the Fraud."

MM: You just thought you might solve some of the mysteries you grew up with?

LS: Exactly. I thought there would be this enormous revelation.

MM: And he was fine knowing you were writing about it for *Esquire*.

LS: He was. I've often wondered why my father allowed me to do those two years' worth of interviews. One thought I've had is that it was a way for him to have his story legitimized. On another level, he simply enjoyed the process of being interviewed. For me, it was almost like we were rebuilding this magical relationship we'd had in my youth.

MM: Because the magical relationship of your youth was based on you listening to his stories. It wasn't ever about you—it was about you listening to him.

LS: That's true. Early in the interview process I remember thinking, I should just press "record" and let him talk. By doing that, this whole other side of my father emerged—a much softer side. It seemed like he was willing to go to the ends of the earth to tell me these interesting stories.

MM: Like any real narcissist, as long as you are paying attention to him on his terms, he'll be willing to play along.

LS: Yes, though I avoided using terms like "narcissist" or "sociopath" in the book; I didn't want a diagnosis to get in the way of the story. But if you look at it from that perspective, I was his "narcissistic supply," no question. It was a very comfortable role for me to be in—it felt totally safe and familiar.

MM: Well, the one way to feel safe with your father is to feed his grandiosity. When he's grandiose, he's benevolent. That's how that personality disorder works. Revisiting your book, I noticed that all your fights with him had to do with asking him questions about what he was doing.

LS: Really? I never noticed that.

MM: You should read your book.

LS: [*Laughs.*] I really should.

MM: Now, when I first met you, I read a very involved, interesting, nicely written version of this book that was just a straight memoir. Why did you change it?

LS: Because I thought it sucked.

MM: Well, I thought it was really riveting, like a detective story.

LS: I wasn't happy with the memoir because I was having so much trouble getting to the emotional truths about my father. Then I came across a box of my childhood cartoons and saw how fearless I'd been. I thought: I might be too afraid to address this stuff about my dad in prose, but I'm not afraid to cartoon the truth.

MM: Let's go back to the source of all this: Your earliest impressions were that he was just the most amazing man ever, who held you spellbound with his stories.

LS: I definitely had an unfettered, pure vision of him as a kid. He was so brilliant, and magical, and filled up the room. But I also have a very early memory, from the third grade or so, of my best friend making a slightly sarcastic comment about my father. I distinctly remember recognizing that maybe some people didn't see my father the same way I did. And it was such a sickening feeling for me. Now people are coming out of the woodwork and saying, "Oh, we knew this all along."

MM: This early period you're talking about—is that when you were doing those childhood cartoons? Because those don't show him bathed in a golden glow.

LS: You're right. I did those between the ages of seven and ten, and they exposed a lot of hard truths about my father: his food addictions, his money problems, his weight issues, his fights with my mother. . . . I saw right through him as a kid. But the more I played his issues up, the more my father loved it. It makes me wonder if he enjoyed being known. I always think about that top FBI agent turned spy, Robert Hanssen. He was regularly selling secrets to the Russians and living a double life as a churchgoing father of six. But nobody really knew him: not the Russians, not his family. He was a total lone wolf. Which reminded me of my dad, because my dad was known by nobody. But he was known by his seven-year-old daughter.

MM: You thought he'd turn out to be a spy, too. Early on, you noticed envelopes with different names on them in your mailbox. And it struck me that this is the perfect era for your dad.

I myself have four different e-mail accounts. On Facebook, I'm Edwin Vacek. And my eBay name is Don Guralnik.

LS: Who's Don Guralnik?

MM: A goldfish I had when I was in college. My roommate and I picked his name out of the phonebook one drunken night of laughing. I'm just thinking about how your dad must be all over everything, because I have three weird names, and I didn't have to do anything except type them in.

LS: Maybe he's deeply involved in a Second Life game.

MM: Why wouldn't he be? It's perfect for him. With all the myths surrounding your dad, would you say he's an intelligent man or a just a really good bullshitter?

LS: Is there really much of a difference?

MM: Yeah. You'd better get a handle on that before you date again.

LS: [*Laughs*.] Don't you think a good bullshitter has to be intelligent?

MM: No. All a good bullshitter needs is an audience that can't tell he's bullshitting.

LS: Well, my father has something of a photographic memory. He has an enormous capacity for retaining historical facts. He can speak very intelligently about politics, religion, economics, and myriad other subjects. And he did teach economics at various universities.

MM: I wonder how many false IDs he had—did you ever look in his wallet?

LS: He had a number of them, as did I—my father made them for me.

MM: Why did your father give you false IDs?

LS: When I was in high school, you could get into the local bars with a college ID. So my father made them for me and my sister, with a laminating machine.

MM: Wow, so he was allowing you to go to bars when you were in high school?

LS: Yeah.

MM: What's *that* all about?

LS: I don't know. That's what I mean about his arbitrary rules: He'd make us fake IDs so we could go to a local bar, but then he'd become enraged when we broke one of his rules. I remember Sylvie was once late for her curfew, and my father drove to the bar where she was hanging out with her boyfriend, marched inside, and dragged her out by her arm, screaming at the bouncer, *"She's only sixteen years old!"*

MM: He was very inconsistent.

LS: Oh, completely.

MM: For a minute I was thinking he was setting you up so he could punish you. But no.

LS: There were a lot of punishments—I was screamed at and grounded all the time. But I didn't know what the rules of my house were—he would make them up as he went along.

MM: That's very upsetting to a kid.

LS: Yeah, it was horrible.

MM: What was your mother's reaction to his inconsistency with you?

LS: She would be playing her cello while he screamed at me, then comfort me after the fact. It was almost like her hands were tied.

MM: Do you know if she came from a childhood where her parents bullied her?

LS: It seems impossible. Her mother was the most wonderful, loving, outgoing woman in the world. Her father was a quiet, upstanding citizen who worked for the government, enforcing the minimum wage in restaurants. She led a very sheltered, Jewish, Long Island upbringing.

MM: I was starting to make up a theory here that your mother let your father bully you because she was so emotionally withholding. That gave her a way to be close to her own kids, because she had somebody there to bully them, and push them toward her, because she couldn't go toward them on her own.

LS: I honestly don't know.

MM: That has to be a childhood dynamic. Do you think she knew the truth about your dad?

LS: I think my mother both knew the truth and was living in denial. Whereas I was always trying to get to the truth and figure out who he was.

MM: These are the kinds of women who turn their backs on going to therapy. They think some mysterious process will happen where a magic wand will hit the person they're married to and they'll wake up and change.

LS: My mother is so unknowable to me, all I can do is speculate. People sometimes ask, "Is your next memoir about your mother?" I could never write a memoir about my mother, because I don't know anything about her. With my dad, there was a paper trail. With my mom, I'd have to get inside her head.

MM: So your mom is as secretive as your dad.

LS: Way *more* secretive. But I don't think there's anything sinister going on; she's just very shy and private.

MM: So both of your parents were in disguise. I'm glad you're seeing a shrink.

LS: [*Laughs.*] I'm glad, too. That's why I'm a halfway normal person.

MM: When did you start to realize your own behavior was becoming self-destructive?

LS: Not until much later. I always looked at the travel, and the stripping, and the lesbian affair as the wild adventures of my youth.

MM: Well, you became the genuine version of your dad's stories. You went out and lived what your dad only pretended to live.

LS: Yeah, in a way I was following in his path, and my sister did the same by going to the Naval Academy.

MM: It's amazing neither of you actually got into the CIA.

LS: It's true. I could have been the vixen who was seducing men with her many languages and disguises, and my sister could have been the gun-toting spy.

MM: That was part of his legacy to you—living large. It was your interpretation of what he gave you, because he didn't have adventures of his own. He was Baron Münchhausen.

LS: He didn't have the adventures he concocted in his mind, but my father has an adventurous spirit; he would have loved to have done that stuff.

MM: If he really wanted to, he would have been doing it. His emotional problems were bigger than his desire to do any of those things. But you did them.

LS: You're right. Maybe it's time to own my accomplishments. Because I've always turned them over to my father, just like everything else.

MM: Your accomplishments are your own. Which brings us to today: Do you still have a relationship with him?

LS: I do not. He stopped talking to me in 2002, when I first discovered he'd lied about his university degrees. Over the years, we've run into each other at family events and had periods of scheduled confrontation—like the time I told him I'd met his stepsister, Elsa, in Argentina—but we've been totally estranged since the book came out.

MM: Are you hoping to reconcile someday?

LS: My hope is not to reconcile with my dad, but to emerge from this experience relatively unscathed. I'd like to be able to have healthy relationships with men, and to continue to grow as a person. There was a time when I used to fantasize about my father and me having a tearful reunion on *Oprah*. But he is not a well man. And at some point you have to ask yourself, what am I getting out of this relationship?

MM: I don't know if he's a narcissist, or a sociopath, or what. A sociopath is defined as someone without a conscience, and it would seem your dad doesn't really have one. He doesn't worry about the consequences of his actions on others—that's a scary kind of person to be around.

LS: It is, and I'm an adult now, so I get to decide who I let into my life. We could talk about this forever, but I think we have enough now.

MM: More than enough!

Questions and topics for discussion

1. Between the ages of seven and ten, Laurie Sandell drew hundreds of cartoons about her father, which she presented to him as gifts. How much did she seem to know about him back then?

2. How would you describe Laurie's early relationship with her father? What went wrong when she turned twelve?

3. Laurie grew up in a home where she was encouraged to keep her family's secrets. Do you think that was a reasonable expectation? What kind of secrets were you asked to keep when you were growing up?

4. How much do you think Laurie's mother knew about her husband's actions? What is a wife's responsibility when it comes to the actions of her partner?

5. While traveling around the world, Laurie had some experiences that were out of character for her: a lesbian fling, giving her passport to a stranger, stripping in Tokyo. What do you think motivated these actions? If you had grown up the way Laurie did, might you have found yourself in similar circumstances?

6. In Part II of the book, Laurie gets a job interviewing celebrities at a top women's magazine. Why do you think she is so good at getting famous people to open up to her?

7. Why was Laurie so dazzled by the celebrities she met? More broadly, why is our society so interested in celebrities?

8. Laurie had a three-year relationship with a screenwriter who lived in L.A. What was at the root of Laurie's issues with Ben?

9. While writing a magazine piece about her father, Laurie started to abuse the sleep aid Ambien. What caused her addiction? What did she learn in rehab that allowed her to get sober?

10. Why do you think Laurie's father attended family week at Shades of Hope when he wasn't on speaking terms with his daughter? Did Laurie's mother somehow force him? Did he secretly wish to support his daughter? Or did he have some other motivation?

11. In recovery, Laurie learned that "secrets keep you sick." How did secrets keep Laurie sick? How did they keep her whole family sick?

12. Laurie's mother told her, "Your first loyalty should be to the family." Do you agree with that statement? What are the circumstances in which "the truth was more important than loyalty," as Laurie insisted?

13. Do you think Laurie's father was mentally ill, a sociopath, brilliant, lonely, or something else entirely? What made him tell all those lies?

14. In many ways, *The Impostor's Daughter* is about the search for an identity. What caused Laurie to lose her identity in the first place? What had to happen before she could find her true self?

15. By the end of the book, has Laurie overcome the challenges of her childhood? What are some new challenges she'll likely have to face?

16. What do you imagine is going to happen to Laurie? Will she find love? Will she ever reconcile with her father? Should she?

17. What other books about truth telling and identity have you read and liked? Were there any particular themes in those books that struck you as similar to the themes in *The Impostor's Daughter*?

Laurie Sandell's suggestions for further reading

Here is a list of my favorite memoirs. Some were written by poets I admire; others by writers who later became friends. One thing I know: There's not a single book on this list that hasn't changed my life in some profound way. I hope you enjoy them as much as I did.

Memoirs

Autobiography of a Face by Lucy Grealy
Tragically, Lucy Grealy died of a heroin overdose in 2002, after a life of myriad operations to fix her jaw, which she partially lost to cancer at the age of nine. It's an unflinching, unsentimental look at a woman's struggle with beauty. Like so many of my favorite memoirists, Grealy was also a poet.

Bereft by Jane Bernstein
Jane is my mother's first cousin. She's the first writer I ever knew, and I happen to be named after her older sister, Laura, whom *Bereft* is about. But that's not why this book is on my list. It's here because it is a devastating, beautifully written account of the murder of Jane's nineteen-year-old sister in 1969, and of her family's ensuing attempt to erase their grief by erasing Laura's memory. It belongs on the shelf next to the best memoirs I've read.

Drinking: A Love Story by Caroline Knapp
Oh, how I love this woman. She, like Lucy Grealy, passed away too soon, dying of lung cancer at age forty-one. I read this book long before I got sober myself, but from the very first sentence, I recognized a kindred spirit in Knapp. The book is about her love affair—and difficult breakup—with alcohol, her struggle with identity, and her

toxic relationships with men. If she were alive, I would write her a stalkerish fan letter.

The Duke of Deception by Geoffrey Wolff
This Boy's Life by Tobias Wolff
Geoffrey and Tobias Wolff are brothers who were split up when their parents divorced: Geoff went to live with their father; Toby lived with their mother. Both ended up writing memoirs. (Note to parents: There is a way to avoid this, but it involves providing your kids with a normal childhood.) I'm partial to *This Boy's Life* because the writing is so damned good, but *The Duke of Deception* is the book that influenced me the most when it came to writing my own memoir. The title alone should tell you why.

A Fan's Notes by Frederick Exley
This book, about the son of a football hero who descends into alcoholism and spends his life in and out of insane asylums, is one of my top five memoirs. As depressing as it can be, it is also frequently hilarious. Exley has a voice like no other.

The Liars' Club by Mary Karr
My favorite memoir—period. This book kills me. Aside from the gorgeous language—Karr is a poet—Karr is able to describe her hardscrabble Texas childhood and deeply flawed parents with empathy, humor, and love. I've read it dozens of times, if only to marvel over her sentences.

Lucky by Alice Sebold
There's no way to sugarcoat this dark story, in which Sebold loses her virginity to a rapist at the age of nineteen. She recovers by confronting her attacker in court, telling the truth to her parents and friends, and writing this stunning memoir. It's a literary and haunting pageturner that predates *The Lovely Bones* but is every bit as compelling.

Stop-Time by Frank Conroy
A classic coming-of-age memoir about a difficult child-

hood, brutal boarding school experience, and wrenching relationship with a distant father.

Truth and Beauty by Ann Patchett
Ann Patchett is one of my favorite writers, but this book, about the author's friendship with Lucy Grealy, is the book of hers that means the most to me. She really shines a light on the joys and complications of a too-close female friendship, and the book adds an extra layer of depth to Lucy's story (if that's even possible). I suggest you read Grealy's book first, then this one.

What Remains by Carole Radziwill
When Carole was writing this book, she took a memoir class I was teaching and used her maiden name—I had no idea who she was! Years later, I became her editor at *Glamour*, and it was then that I read this extraordinary book, which chronicles her blue-collar upbringing and start in journalism, followed by the death of her husband and two closest friends. Her book became an extremely important touchstone for me as I worked on my own memoir.

When Skateboards Will Be Free by Saïd Sayrafiezadeh
I first met Saïd in the coffee shop where I write. Now we call ourselves "coworkers," because we write together every day. I was blown away by this book about his experience growing up in the Socialist Workers Party and—surprise, surprise—difficult relationship with his father. If you think I'm just giving a plug to a friend, don't listen to me; listen to Dwight Garner of the *New York Times*, who chose *When Skateboards Will Be Free* as one of his Top 10 Books of 2009.

Graphic Memoirs

Blankets by Craig Thompson
I met Craig Thompson when I spent a summer in Portland, Oregon, putting the finishing touches on my book. I was already a huge fan of his astonishing six-hundred-page memoir, which chronicled his Evangelical Christian upbringing and experience of first love. In fact, I loved his book so much I was terrified to meet him, but he turned out to be a wonderful person, which made me adore this book even more. Read it for the layered and complex story, then revisit it for the art. It will take your breath away.

Fun Home by Alison Bechdel
Several people have compared my book to this memoir about a young girl's sexual awakening and complicated relationship with her gay, closeted father. And I take that as a huge compliment, since this book is just brilliant.

Maus I and *Maus II* by Art Spiegelman
The first graphic novels I ever read were these two, about Spiegelman's father, a Holocaust survivor. Using mice and cats as metaphors for Jews and Nazis, Spiegelman chronicles his father's experience in the camps, and his own fractured relationship with his broken father. These book are *the* classics of the genre.

Persepolis by Marjane Satrapi
Satrapi's first Persepolis book chronicles her early life during the Islamic Revolution, when the veil was reintroduced as a religious requirement for women. Her stark, black-and-white drawings are deceptively simple—the story is not.

Part I

SECRETS

WHENEVER MY FATHER WENT OUT OF TOWN, HE HAD THE MAIL STOPPED. IT DIDN'T MATTER IF HE WAS GONE FOR ONE, TWO, OR TEN DAYS — IF MY FATHER WASN'T HOME, THE MAIL DIDN'T COME.

I WONDERED WHAT MADE HIM GUARD THE MAIL SO JEALOUSLY. HIS EXPLANATIONS DIDN'T MAKE SENSE.

ACH, IT'S ALL JUNK MAIL, SEE?

STONEMAN COLLEGE BOOKSTORE

BUT THERE *IS* NO "STONEMAN COLLEGE."

A-*HA*! I KNOW THAT, AND YOU KNOW THAT, BUT *THEY* DON'T KNOW THAT.

THE FEW TIMES I MANAGED TO INTERCEPT THE MAIL, I FOUND THAT EVERY LETTER IN THE PILE WAS ADDRESSED TO A DIFFERENT NAME.

EVERY NOW AND THEN, THESE STRANGE NAMES WOULD POP UP ON THE OTHER END OF THE PHONE.

IS WINSTON RAMBLEAU THERE?

WRONG NUMBER.

LATER THAT NIGHT...

WHO CALLED? THAT WAS FOR ME, DAMMIT!

AFTER THAT, WHATEVER NAME THEY GAVE, I JUST YELLED FOR MY DAD.

IT'S FOR YOU!

I GREW UP IN CALIFORNIA IN A HOUSE AT THE END OF A CUL-DE-SAC ON A WIDE, SMOOTH STREET. I WAS THE OLDEST OF THREE GIRLS.

FROM THE OUTSIDE, OUR HOUSE LOOKED PRETTY MUNDANE.

NOT SO ON THE INSIDE.

THIS ONE'S A BEAUT—IT'S A MNANDI KNIFE WITH GIRAFFE BONE INLAY.

BILL!

MY FATHER WAS A PROFESSOR OF ECONOMICS AT THE UNIVERSITY OF THE PACIFIC IN STOCKTON, CALIFORNIA. I WOULD GO TO CLASS WITH HIM ON OCCASION AND SIT IN THE BACK ROW WHILE HE PACED IN FRONT OF THE LECTERN, STOPPING EVERY FEW MINUTES TO WIPE HIS SWEATY FOREHEAD WITH A FOLDED HANDKERCHIEF.

HIS STUDENTS SEEMED TERRIFIED OF HIM, BUT TO ME HE JUST LOOKED STRONG AND HANDSOME — LIKE AN ITALIAN TENOR — WITH HIS GENEROUS GUT AND HIS THICK BLACK HAIR SWEPT INTO A POMPADOUR.

DURING MIDTERMS, I KEPT MY FATHER COMPANY AT THE KITCHEN TABLE WHILE HE GRADED EXAMS.

I WOULD CERTAINLY NEVER HAVE SECOND-GUESSED **HIM**.

HE MAINTAINED A LIBRARY OF ELEVEN THOUSAND BOOKS. HE'D READ THEM ALL. ANYTHING I WANTED TO KNOW ABOUT, HE SIMPLY WALKED OVER TO A SHELF, PULLED A BOOK DOWN, THEN FLIPPED IT OPEN TO THE EXACT PAGE THAT SHOWED HIS POINT.

THIS ONE.

BUT HE WASN'T JUST BOOK SMART. HE WAS A BONA FIDE GENIUS.

IT'S AN ORGANIZATION CALLED MENSA, AND YES, YOUR FATHER IS A MEMBER. BY QUITE A FEW POINTS.

HE'D GRADUATED NUMBER ONE IN HIS CLASS FROM THE UNIVERSITY OF BUENOS AIRES.

THE STUPIDEST THING I EVER DID WAS SELL THAT MEDAL. IT WAS SOLID GOLD.

IF YOU EVER GET IT BACK, CAN I HAVE IT?

HE'D GOTTEN A LAW DEGREE FROM NYU, A PHD FROM COLUMBIA, AND HAD TAUGHT AT STANFORD.

WRITTEN POSITION PAPERS FOR KISSINGER.

SAT ON THE NATIONAL SECURITY COUNCIL.

HE COULD ALSO IDENTIFY EVERY PIECE OF CLASSICAL MUSIC THAT EXISTED.

7

WHERE ALL THIS TALENT CAME FROM, I HAD NO IDEA. MY FATHER WAS ESTRANGED FROM HIS ENTIRE FAMILY. WHEN PRESSED, HE SPOKE OF THEM WITH VENOM— PARTICULARLY HIS STEPSISTER, ELSA, WHOM HIS FATHER ADOPTED AFTER MARRYING HER MOTHER.

SHE WAS **HORRIBLE.** A WITCH.

THE ONE EXCEPTION WAS HIS LATE FATHER— A STRICT, GERMAN TASKMASTER—WHOM HE WORSHIPPED.

HE WAS A TWENTY-FOUR-HOUR TEACHING MACHINE. BY THE TIME I WAS YOUR AGE, I KNEW EVERY CAPITAL OF EVERY COUNTRY IN THE WORLD.

WHEN I WAS FIVE I STARTED PIANO LESSONS. MY FATHER OFTEN STOOD IN THE DOORWAY, LISTENING. IF I PLAYED A SCALE PERFECTLY, HIS PRAISE WAS SO EFFUSIVE I WANTED TO TAKE A BATH IN IT.

I SWEAR TO GOD, BEETHOVEN COULDN'T HAVE PLAYED THAT SCALE BETTER.

8

WHEN HE WAS SIMPLY SILENT, I KNEW I'D LET HIM DOWN.

HE WAS LIKE ONE OF THOSE AVUN-CULAR RUSSIAN GYMNASTICS COACHES I'D SEEN ON TV DURING THE OLYMPICS:

HOISTING THEIR CHARGES INTO THE AIR WHEN THEY'D COMPLETED A FEAT OF GYM-NASTIC PERFECTION.

POST-PIANO RECITAL

THAT LITTLE JAPANESE KID WAS ABSOLUTELY **BRILLIANT.**

PROGRAM

TURNING AWAY WHEN THEY'D FAILED.

MY MOTHER TRIED TO MAKE UP FOR MY FATHER'S JUDGMENTS.

YOU'VE NEVER PLAYED THE THIRD MOVEMENT BETTER, I SWEAR.

BUT HER WORDS MEANT LITTLE TO ME. IT WAS MY FATHER'S PRAISE I CRAVED.

WHATEVER.

THE THING IS, HE DID THINGS BETTER THAN ANYONE ELSE.

SCHOOL SCIENCE PROJECT

I WANTED TO BE THE BEST TOO. AND WITH HIS HELP, I ALWAYS WAS.

BRAVO!

COUNTY SCIENC

ZING

Stories and Gifts

AS EARLY AS KINDERGARTEN, I REMEMBER MY FATHER TRAVELING, SOMETIMES FOR MONTHS AT A TIME. HE RARELY GAVE US NOTICE.

SO WE COULD COMMUNICATE WITH HIM WHILE HE WAS AWAY, MY FATHER SET UP HAM RADIO EQUIPMENT, WHICH WAS ALWAYS ON, IN THE DEN.

I WOULD BE SITTING ON THE COUCH, WATCHING TV, AND THE CRACKLING WOULD GROW LOUDER, PUNCTUATED BY MY FATHER'S DEEP, GRAVELLY BARITONE.

HE WOULD RETURN AS SUDDENLY AS HE'D LEFT.

DADDY!!!

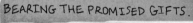

BEARING THE PROMISED GIFTS.

WHATEVER PAIN I HAD FELT IN MY FATHER'S ABSENCE VANISHED THE MINUTE HE FLIPPED OPEN THE LID OF THAT SUITCASE.

THAT NIGHT AT DINNER...

WHAT WAS PANAMA LIKE?

IT WAS VERY WET—AND THE HEAT WAS HORRENDOUS. THE MOSQUITOES, I SWEAR TO YOU, SOME OF THEM WERE THE SIZE OF YOUR HAND.

HE TOLD US ABOUT THE WOODEN HOUSES OF THE SHANTYTOWNS, WHICH CLUNG TO THE SIDE OF A MOUNTAIN.

ABOUT A TRIP HE'D TAKEN IN A MOTORIZED CANOE, AFTER WHICH HE'D HIKED THROUGH WAIST-DEEP MUD TO A HIDDEN LOCATION.

HOW HE'D SEEN JEWELS THAT SPARKLED LIKE MERCURY, AND ONE TEARDROP-SHAPED STONE AS BIG AS THE HOPE DIAMOND.

JUST LIKE THAT, HE WAS BACK IN OUR LIVES.

MORE!

SHH... TOMORROW.

WHEN I WAS SIX I FOUND A VELVET CASE IN A BOX IN THE ATTIC.

I CARRIED THE CASE DOWNSTAIRS TO MY FATHER, AND HE GREW MISTY-EYED.

THAT LED TO HOURS OF THE MOST RIVETING STORIES I'D EVER HEARD.

BULLETS WERE COMING FROM EVERYWHERE— ALL OF A SUDDEN, SOMEBODY YELLS, GRENADE!

OVER THE NEXT FEW DAYS, WE DISAPPEARED INTO THE DEN FOR CONVERSATIONS THAT LASTED FOR HOURS.

DO YOU WANT HER TO REPEAT THESE STORIES AT SCHOOL?

AY, LEAVE US BE FOR JUST TEN MINUTES!

I WON'T.

HOURS LATER...

I DON'T KNOW IF THEY HAD ORDERS TO BUMP ME OR NOT—BUT I MADE IT ALIVE TO LA PAZ.

14

THE MAN SAID, "LADIES AND GENTLEMEN, I HAVE THE PAINFUL DUTY TO INFORM YOU THAT DOÑA MARIA EVA DUARTE DE PERÓN HAS DIED. I JUMPED TEN FEET IN THE AIR AND YELLED, *THE WHORE IS DEAD! THE WHORE IS DEAD!* MY COUSIN RUTH GRABBED MY ARM, BUT IT WAS TOO LATE: I ENDED UP IN PRISON.

I WAS PROUD TO BE THE DAUGHTER OF SUCH A BRAVE MAN.

THE WHORE IS DEAD!

EVERY ONCE IN A WHILE, MY FATHER WOULD GIVE ME A GIFT, A SPECIAL TREASURE.

THIS WOODEN SWORD IS MORE THAN TWO HUNDRED YEARS OLD.

THE NEXT DAY, I WOULD BRING THESE PRESENTS TO SCHOOL FOR SHOW-AND-TELL.

DEEP WITHIN THE PERUVIAN JUNGLE, THE NATIVES WIELD THIS SWORD.

PEOPLE CELEBRATE THE IMAGINATION OF A CHILD, BUT I FOUND MY CLASSMATES' OBSERVATIONS TO BE WHOLLY UNINSPIRING.

EVEN THEN, I WAS DRAWN TO COMPELLING, LARGER-THAN-LIFE PERSONALITIES.

VISIONS

WHEN I TURNED SEVEN, MY MOTHER ENROLLED ME IN THE BROWNIES. I WAS GIVEN A LIGHT BROWN JUMPER, A CRISP WHITE SHIRT, AND A DARK BROWN BEANIE.

HMMM...

A FEW DAYS LATER...

THIS IS A FITNESS LIFESTYLE BADGE. THIS IS A YEAR PIN.

I THINK YOU HAVE TO **EARN** THESE.

SALVATION ARMY

AY, **HIJA**, YOU **DID** EARN THEM.

THE AWARDS GLEAMED ON MY CHEST. MY FATHER GAZED AT ME PROUDLY. IN THE MIRROR I SAW A BROWNIE WHO HAD PASSED EVERY TEST, ACCOMPLISHED EVERY GOAL. PERHAPS I **HAD** EARNED THEM.

AROUND THAT TIME, I STARTED DRAWING CARTOONS. MY MATERNAL GRANDFATHER, WHO LIKED TO PAINT AND SKETCH, TAUGHT ME HOW.

MY FIRST DRAWINGS WERE PEACEFUL INTERPRETATIONS OF RURAL LIFE. *

BUT SOON, I WAS ON TO DARKER TABLEAUX, CARTOONS I DREW EXCLUSIVELY FOR MY FATHER. IN EACH DRAWING, HIS HEAD WAS HUGE; OUTRAGEOUSLY OUT OF PROPORTION TO THE REST OF HIS BODY. FOR COMIC FLOURISH, I ADDED A GIANT WART ON THE TIP OF HIS NOSE.

* ACTUAL DRAWINGS.

18

WHEN FINISHED, I WOULD PROP THE CARTOON ON A STATUE CALLED **VISIONS** THAT MY PARENTS KEPT ON A CREDENZA IN THE HALLWAY.

HIDING BEHIND THE BASEMENT DOOR, I'D WAIT FOR MY FATHER TO FIND IT. SOMETIMES I HAD TO WAIT FOR LONG PERIODS.

EVENTUALLY, I'D HEAR HIS FOOT-STEPS IN THE HALL, FAINT AT FIRST, THEN LOUDER. THE HAMMERING IN MY HEART WOULD QUICKEN WITH EVERY STEP.

PRICELESS. THIS IS **PRICELESS.**

19

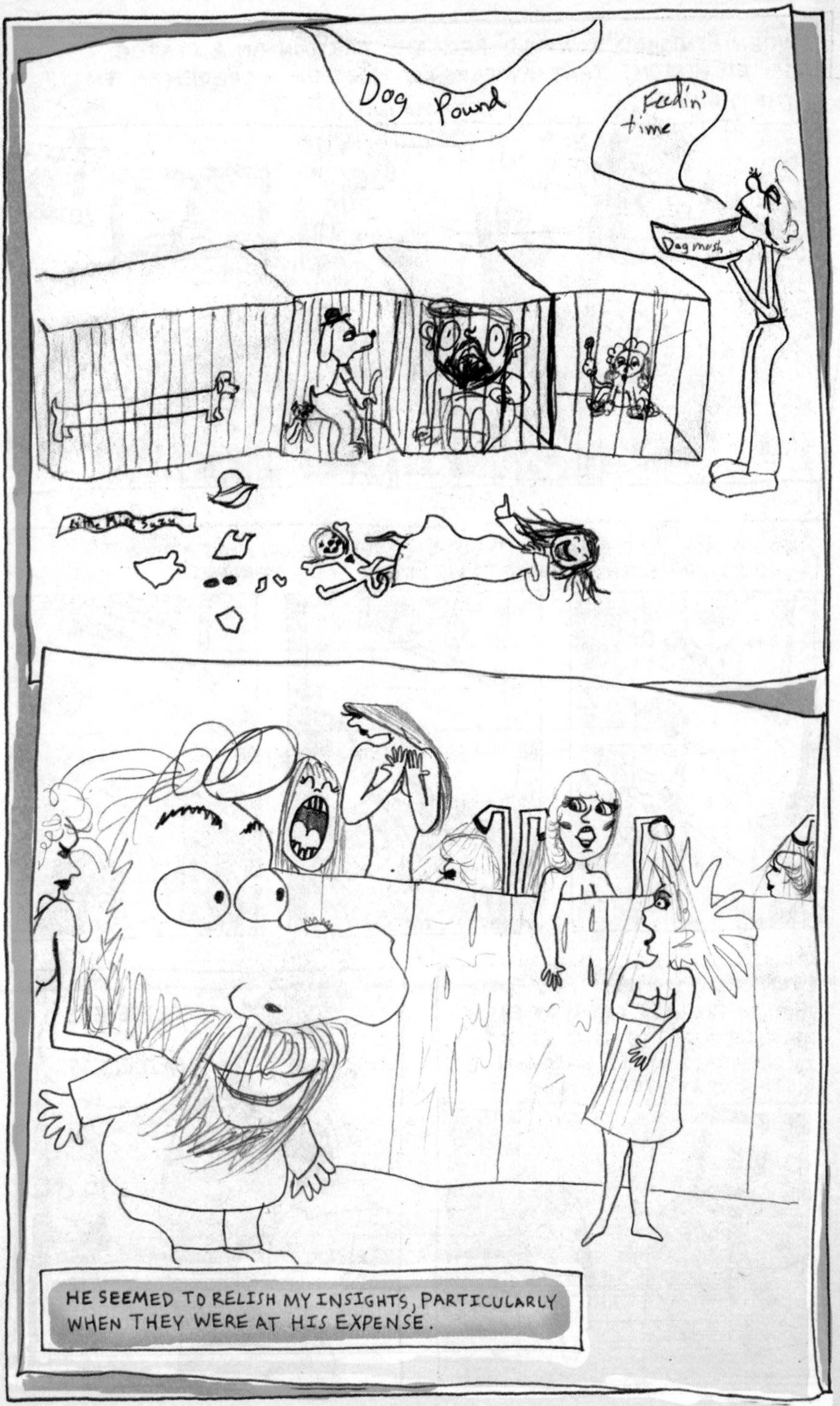
Dog Pound
Feedin' time
Dog mush
HE SEEMED TO RELISH MY INSIGHTS, PARTICULARLY WHEN THEY WERE AT HIS EXPENSE.

HE'D TAKE THE NEWEST DRAWING AND ADD IT TO A RAPIDLY GROWING PILE IN AN ORANGE CARDBOARD BOX. EVENTUALLY, THERE WERE MORE THAN TWO HUNDRED OF THEM. THEY SAT IN THE ATTIC, COLLECTING DUST. I CONTINUED TO DRAW.

A SURPRISE MOVE

ONE DAY, MY FATHER CAME HOME AND CALLED A FAMILY MEETING. WE ASSEMBLED IN THE DEN. MY MOTHER SAT ON THE SOFA, HOLDING MY THREE-YEAR-OLD SISTER, SYLVIE. KARYN AND I SHARED THE HASSOCK.

WE'RE MOVING TO NEW YORK.

HOORAY!

ONE MINUTE, IT SEEMED, WE WERE PLAYING OUTSIDE, CATCHING FIREFLIES IN JARS.

THE NEXT WE WERE PULLING INTO MY AUNT'S DRIVEWAY.

A FEW WEEKS LATER, WE MOVED INTO THE TOP FLOOR OF A TWO-FAMILY HOUSE ON AN UNREMARKABLE STREET.

MY SISTERS AND I ALL SHARED A ROOM, AND KARYN AND SYLVIE SCRAMBLED TO DO MY BIDDING.

THERE WAS AN UNSPOKEN RULE IN OUR FAMILY: EVERYONE IN THE HOUSE SERVED MY FATHER, AND MY SISTERS SERVED ME.

MY FATHER REINFORCED MY BELIEF THAT I DESERVED TO BE RUNNING A MINI-EMPIRE.

ONLY I KNEW THE REAL REASON WHY.

YES, YOU'RE MY FAVORITE. BUT THAT'S JUST BETWEEN US, *CAPISCE*?

WHICH ONE IS BETTER?

THAT ONE.

ABOUT A MONTH AFTER WE MOVED, MY FATHER STARTED HIS NEW JOB AS A PROFESSOR AT A LOCAL COLLEGE.

THE MONEY IS MUCH BETTER, BUT THIS PLACE IS NO STANFORD. THE LEVEL OF INTELLECT— *NIGHT* AND *DAY*.

HE HIRED A SECRETARY NAMED GIULIA TO WORK IN HIS OFFICE. GIULIA SAT AT ONE OF THE DESKS, MANNING THE PHONE, AND MY FATHER SAT AT THE OTHER, GRADING PAPERS AND TYPING UP MEMOS.

I ADORED GIULIA. SHE SPOKE IN THE HIGH-PITCHED VOICE OF A LITTLE GIRL, SMELLED OF LOVE'S BABY SOFT PERFUME, AND WORE HER HAIR LONG, IN RIPPLING BLACK WAVES.

I DREW HER OFTEN — SHE WAS SOMETHING OF A MUSE.

ABOUT ONCE A MONTH, GIULIA CAME TO OUR HOUSE TO TAKE MY SISTERS AND ME TO DINNER, A MOVIE, OR AN AMUSEMENT PARK.

GIULIA IS HERE!

SHE BOUGHT US WHATEVER WE WANTED — AND WE TOOK FULL ADVANTAGE OF HER GENEROSITY.

Playlan

THAT ONE!

25

WE'D RETURN HOME LADEN WITH GIFTS AND BRIMMING WITH STORIES.

SHE LETS US EAT COTTON CANDY BEFORE DINNER— WHY WON'T **YOU?**

AS FAR AS I COULD TELL, MY MOTHER WASN'T THE LEAST BIT CONCERNED ABOUT GIULIA'S CLOSE RELATIONSHIP WITH HER CHILDREN.

WOW, SHE BOUGHT YOU THAT TOO?

THOUGH I SEEM TO HAVE BEEN DISTURBED ON HER BEHALF.

To my arthritis-stricken mother

SIGNS /////

ONE DAY, MY FATHER ASKED IF I WANTED TO GO INTO THE CITY.

ARE YOU READY TO SEE NEW YORK?

YES!

I WANT TO GO TOO.

MY FATHER AND I WENT TO THE UNITED NATIONS. I WAS IMPRESSED BY THE PHOTOS OF AMBASSADORS THAT LINED THE LONG HALLWAYS.

27

AT LUNCHTIME, WE ATE IN THE DELEGATES DINING ROOM.

SHE'S TWELVE, OF COURSE?

OF COURSE.

TEN YEARS OLD →

AN AMBASSADOR WAS EATING LUNCH JUST A FEW TABLES AWAY.

YOU SEE THAT ELEGANT-LOOKING MAN IN THE SUIT? THAT'S AMBASSADOR YOUSEF MAHMOUD OF BURUNDI.

MY FATHER LIFTED HIS WATER GLASS IN THE MAN'S DIRECTION.

WE ENDED THE DAY WITH A MOVIE AT RADIO CITY MUSIC HALL AND A CARRIAGE RIDE AROUND CENTRAL PARK. I LEANED AGAINST MY FATHER'S SCRATCHY SHIRT AND FELT MY EYES START TO CLOSE. AS LONG AS HE WAS THERE, I FELT SAFE.

A FEW WEEKS LATER, MY FATHER CALLED US INTO THE LIVING ROOM FOR ANOTHER FAMILY MEETING.

I'M LEAVING MY TEACHING POSITION TO PURSUE SOME PERSONAL VENTURES.

THE LIBERALS AT SCHOOL HATE DADDY BECAUSE HE'S A CONSERVATIVE.

I DIDN'T KNOW WHAT A CONSERVATIVE WAS, BUT I HAD HEARD MY FATHER SAY THE WORD ENOUGH TO KNOW THAT THEY — LIKE THE JEWS — WERE THE CHOSEN PEOPLE.

I HAD A VAGUE VISION OF A GROUP OF BLAND, NONDESCRIPT MEN OUT TO GET MY FATHER.

LIBERAL LIBERAL LIBERAL LIBERAL

WE MOVED AGAIN, TO A BIG FOUR-BEDROOM HOUSE IN BRONXVILLE, ONE TOWN AWAY FROM MY AUNT.

DAD **ALWAYS** MAKES US MOVE!

IN THE NEW HOUSE, YOU'LL HAVE YOUR OWN ROOM. TRUST ME — IT'S EVEN BETTER.

29

MY MOTHER RETURNED TO WORK AS A FIRST-GRADE TEACHER, DRIVING OFF EACH MORNING IN HER WHITE FORD TAURUS.

MY FATHER WAS THERE TO TAKE CARE OF US INSTEAD. HE SPENT MOST OF HIS TIME SPRUCING UP OUR NEW HOME.

AND TALKING TO US ABOUT DEALS HE HAD IN THE WORKS.

IF I SELL THIS TECHNOLOGY IN A PERIOD OF TWO YEARS, I WILL GET TEN PERCENT OF THE SALE. SO WHAT'S TEN PERCENT OF A HUNDRED MILLION DOLLARS? RIIIGHT.

BUT UNLIKE MY FRIENDS' FATHERS, HE DIDN'T GO TO WORK. HE SLEPT UNTIL NOON AND DIDN'T BOTHER TO GET DRESSED, WEARING HIS BOXER SHORTS AND AN UNDERSHIRT ALL DAY LONG.

WHAT TIME IS IT?

ALMOST ONE O'CLOCK!

I MADE EGGS.

SOMETIMES HE FELL INTO A BLACK, UNREACHABLE HOLE FOR THE DAY.

LOOK, I MADE YOU— WHAT'S WRONG?

I'M A FAILURE.

WHEN I TURNED TWELVE, SOMETHING CHANGED IN OUR RELATIONSHIP.

WHERE...IS...MY... STAPLER?!

I DIDN'T KNOW WHAT I'D DONE TO MAKE HIM SO ANGRY, OR HOW I'D LOST MY IMMUNITY IN THE HOUSEHOLD.

BILL— TAKE IT TO THE BASEMENT!

I WAS TOO PROUD TO COVER MY EARS. BUT THE NOISE WAS SO LOUD, IT GAVE ME HEADACHES.

MONSTER!

IDIOT!

ONCE WE WENT DOWNSTAIRS, MY MOTHER SEEMED NOT TO HEAR IT AT ALL, THOUGH I COULD STILL HEAR HER MUSIC; IT WAS A SOUNDTRACK TO OUR FIGHTS.

AFTERWARD, I ALWAYS APOLOGIZED. I KNEW I'D SOMEHOW PROVOKED MY FATHER — AND I DIDN'T HAVE HIS STAMINA FOR HOLDING A GRUDGE.

WERE WE ALIKE? I LIKED TO THINK SO.

LATER THAT DAY...

33

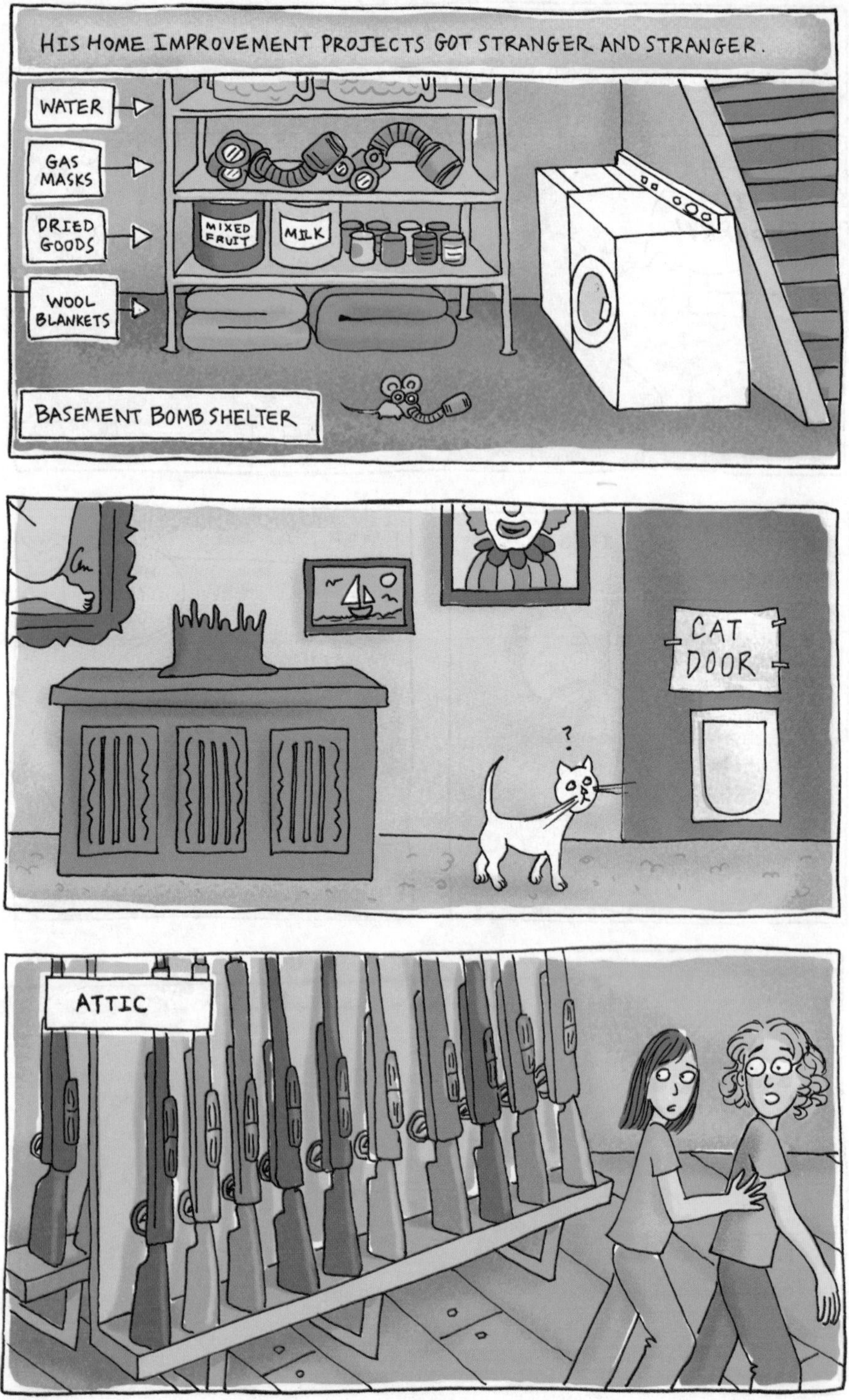
HIS HOME IMPROVEMENT PROJECTS GOT STRANGER AND STRANGER.
WATER
GAS MASKS
DRIED GOODS
WOOL BLANKETS
MIXED FRUIT
MILK
BASEMENT BOMB SHELTER
CAT DOOR
?
ATTIC

FOR THE MOST PART HE STAYED OUT OF THE WAY, ALONE, LOCKED IN HIS BEDROOM WITH THE TELEVISION ON AT FULL BLAST. BUT HE HAD ONE RITUAL YOU COULD SET YOUR WATCH BY.

M.A.S.H. WILL BE RIGHT BACK AFTER THESE MESSAGES...

EVERY DAY, HE WOULD LISTEN FOR THE SOUND OF THE MAILTRUCK PULLING INTO OUR DRIVEWAY. THEN HE WOULD RACE DOWNSTAIRS TO THE FRONT DOOR, GRAB A THICK STACK OF LETTERS, AND LOCK HIMSELF IN THE DEN.

THROUGH THE SLATS IN THE DOOR, I COULD SEE HIM SLICE THROUGH THE ENVELOPES WITH SURGICAL PRECISION.

AFTER, HE WOULD BRING DOZENS OF
LETTERS INTO THE KITCHEN AND THROW
THEM IN THE GARBAGE, STEPPING
INTO THE CAN AND BOUNCING UP
AND DOWN ON ONE FOOT UNTIL
THE MAIL WAS SMASHED FLAT.

AND TAKE THE BAG TO THE CURB.

I KNEW MY FATHER WAS STRANGE, NOT LIKE OTHER DADS I KNEW.

BUT MOST OF THE TIME, I THOUGHT THEY WERE STRANGE AND
WE WERE THE NORMAL ONES.

DAMMIT,
I TOLD YOU
NOT TO CHANGE
THE CHANNEL!

BY THE TIME I WAS IN HIGH SCHOOL, THOUGH, I KNEW JUST HOW DIFFERENT WE WERE. I RARELY BROUGHT FRIENDS HOME. I COULDN'T RISK IT.

JESUS, DAD, WILL YOU PUT ON SOME CLOTHES ?!?

WHAT — I CAN'T BE COMFORTABLE IN MY *OWN HOME* ?

THE AIR WAS THICK WITH NEGATIVITY. KARYN AND I, WHO'D NEVER SO MUCH AS BICKERED, STARTED TO HAVE MASSIVE FIGHTS.

BASKIN ROBBINS

THOSE ARE *MINE*!

HELP! HELP!

MY FATHER REPLACED THE LOCKS ON THE DOORKNOBS WITH COMBINATION LOCKS — ON THE *OUTSIDE* OF OUR DOORS.

IS THAT SO YOU CAN LOCK US IN?

DON'T BE RIDICULOUS — IT'S SO YOU CAN'T STEAL EACH OTHER'S CLOTHES.

THERE WAS NO PRIVACY, NO BOUNDARIES.

OH! SORRY.

DAD!

MY FATHER BECAME APOPLECTIC WHEN HE CAUGHT ME WATCHING A MADONNA VIDEO, AND BANNED MTV FROM OUR HOME.

I WILL *NOT* TOLERATE THIS *FILTH* IN MY HOUSE!

IT'S JUST "LIKE A VIRGIN"!

HE WROTE AN ESSAY IN SYLVIE'S NAME AND PUBLISHED IT IN HER SIXTH GRADE LITERARY MAGAZINE. SHE FOUND OUT ONLY WHEN A CLASSMATE COMPLIMENTED HER ON HER WRITING SKILLS.

SHATTERED GLASS AND A FEW BROKEN *PIECES* BY SYLVIE SANDELL. NOTE: MY DADDY HELPED ME WRITE THIS STORY.

I'M NEVER GOING BACK— *EVER*!!!

WHAT IF DAD IS JUST *INSANE*?

HE'S NOT. HE'S A GOOD WRITER AND WANTED TO BE PUBLISHED SOMEWHERE.

LATER THAT DAY...

WHAT DOES HE EVEN *DO* WITH HIS LIFE?

I TOLD YOU: HE SETS UP COMPUTER SYSTEMS FOR FOREIGN GOVERNMENTS.

BUT WHAT DOES THAT MEAN?

DEALS! HE IS MAKING DEALS. NOW STOP ASKING.

I DID STOP ASKING. I TRIED TO CREATE A NORMAL EXISTENCE OUTSIDE MY HOME: DATING THE STAR OF THE BASKETBALL TEAM, ATTENDING MY JUNIOR PROM WITH A NICE JEWISH BOY.

Laurie and date, Gordon Stein 6-2-88

IT DIDN'T WORK. BY MY SENIOR YEAR OF HIGH SCHOOL, I COULDN'T WAIT TO GET AWAY FROM HIM.

KNOCK. KNOCK. KNOCK.

WHAT.

MADONNA LIKE A

KARYN WAS PLANNING HER OWN ESCAPE: SHE APPLIED EARLY ADMISSION TO THE U.S. NAVAL ACADEMY AND GOT IN.

SIX-MINUTE MILE.

BUT THEN MY FATHER AND I WOULD FALL INTO ONE OF OUR MARATHON LATE-NIGHT CONVERSATIONS, AND HE WOULD TELL ME THINGS HE'D NEVER EVEN TOLD MY MOTHER, AND I WOULD FEEL CLOSE TO HIM AGAIN.

MY FATHER HAD SEVERAL HORSES, SERVANTS— NOW THIS WAS A MAN WHO KNEW HOW TO **LIVE**. MY MOTHER WAS A LITTLE... YOU KNOW, CUCKOO. SHE ONCE PEED ON THE SIDEWALK AFTER SHE DRANK TOO MUCH AT A PARTY.

OTHER SECRETS CAME OUT. I LEARNED MY FATHER HAD CHANGED HIS LAST NAME FROM SCHMIDT TO SANDELL.

WHY?

OH, IT WAS DIFFICULT TO PRONOUNCE.

WHEN I WAS EIGHTEEN, I LEARNED MY GRANDFATHER HAD KILLED HIMSELF. MY MOTHER SLIPPED— SHE HADN'T MEANT TO TELL ME.

BUT WHY WOULD YOU **KEEP** THAT FROM ME?

BECAUSE IT'S PAINFUL, DARLING.

I LOVED HIM WITH INTENSITY. I HATED HIM WITH INTENSITY. THERE WAS NO MIDDLE GROUND.

A DISCOVERY

6573 8225
MEMBER SINCE 1984
LAURIE A. SANDE

NOVEMBER 1992

ONE THANKSGIVING, I CAME HOME FROM COLLEGE TO FIND THAT MY FATHER HAD TURNED MY BEDROOM INTO AN OFFICE.

HE'D COVERED AN ENTIRE WALL WITH HAM RADIO EQUIPMENT, WHICH LOOKED LIKE THE INSIDE OF A SUBMARINE, COMPLETE WITH BLINKING LIGHTS, KNOBS, DIALS, ANTENNAE, AND MICRO-PHONES.

PRINTS BY MIRÓ AND PICASSO — OR SO HE SAID — WERE STACKED UP AGAINST ONE WALL. HIS LATEST CLAIM WAS THAT HE'D TAKEN UP ART DEALING, BUT MY HUNCH WAS THAT HE WAS IN THE CIA.

41

ON THE LAST DAY OF MY VISIT, I PEEKED AT THE FILES THAT COVERED HIS DESK.

LAURIE'S MISCELLANEOUS PAPERS

EUROPE TRIP!!!

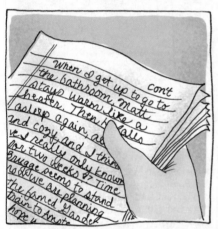

WHEN MY FATHER GOT HOME FROM THE GYM, I POUNCED.

YOU PHOTOCOPIED MY *DIARY*?!

42

I WAS SAVING THIS FOR YOU- IN CASE YOU LOST IT!
HE THEN STORMED OUT OF THE ROOM.
LEAVING ME ALONE, FEELING FURIOUS AND VIOLATED...
BUT NOT ENTIRELY SURE HE WASN'T TELLING THE TRUTH.

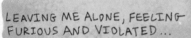

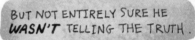

I RETURNED TO SCHOOL AND JOINED A SORORITY. IT WAS THE MOST NORMAL THING I COULD THINK OF TO DO.

AT TWENTY-ONE, I LOST MY VIRGINITY, TO A DISTANT, BEAUTIFUL COMPOSER. HE WAS THE POLAR OPPOSITE OF MY FATHER, SO I HAD NO IDEA HOW TO REACH HIM.

UM... DID YOU SLEEP OK?

AFTER COLLEGE, I HAD A TORTUROUS BREAKUP WITH THE COMPOSER AND MOVED BACK HOME. NOT MUCH HAD CHANGED: MY FATHER STILL SAT AROUND IN HIS UNDERWEAR, WAITED FOR THE MAIL, AND LOCKED HIMSELF IN HIS OFFICE WITH THE TELEVISION AT FULL BLAST.

WHAT?

NOTHING.

ONE SATURDAY I HAPPENED TO CATCH THE MAILMAN FIRST.

I'D NEVER HAD A CREDIT CARD BEFORE. I HAD NO IDEA THEY JUST SENT THEM TO YOU. I DECIDED I'D USE IT TO BUY A MOUNTAIN BIKE.

44

LATER, I FOUND MY DAD IN THE KITCHEN. HE WAS LOOKING THROUGH THE REFRIGERATOR FOR HIS "POTION," A MIXTURE OF FRUIT JUICE AND SODA.

DAD?

DON'T SCARE ME LIKE THAT!

SORRY, I JUST WANTED TO SHOW YOU SOMETHING. LOOK WHAT DISCOVER SENT ME.

THAT IS *MINE*!

BUT *MY* NAME IS ON THE CARD!

I OPENED IT ON YOUR BEHALF TO HELP YOU BUILD UP YOUR CREDIT. NOW GIVE IT TO ME!

I WAS FURIOUS BECAUSE I REALLY WANTED THE MOUNTAIN BIKE, NOT BECAUSE I SUSPECTED HE'D DONE SOMETHING WRONG.

LOOK, I'LL CUT IT UP IN FRONT OF YOU.

I SURRENDERED THE CARD AND WATCHED AS HE CUT IT INTO A DOZEN TINY PIECES.

45

A YEAR LATER, I WAS LIVING IN CHICAGO, WORKING AS A WAITRESS, AND WAS IN MY FAVORITE STORE, WONDERING HOW I COULD BUY A PAIR OF SHOES I COULDN'T AFFORD.

I WENT OUTSIDE TO CALL DISCOVER FROM A PAY PHONE.

THERE WAS A LONG PAUSE, INTERMITTENT TYPING.

SHE PUT ME ON HOLD, I HEARD SOME LIGHT JAZZ, AND THEN...

I CALLED MY MOTHER.

WHY ARE YOU CRYING? CALM DOWN — I CAN'T HEAR YOU!

WHEN I FINALLY COMPOSED MYSELF ENOUGH TO TELL HER WHAT WAS GOING ON, SHE GREW QUIET. SHE DIDN'T ATTEMPT TO DEFEND MY FATHER OR SAY THERE HAD BEEN A MISUNDERSTANDING.

I NEED TO TALK TO DADDY.

AN HOUR LATER, SHE CALLED BACK, SOUNDING SUBDUED.

YOUR FATHER FEELS TERRIBLE, LAURIE. HE KNOWS WHAT HE DID WAS WRONG.

BUT I HAVE TO LIVE WITH THE CONSEQUENCES — MY CREDIT IS PROBABLY RUINED!

I'LL TAKE OUT A LOAN. I'LL PAY OFF THE CARD. IT WON'T AFFECT YOUR CREDIT.

LET ME SPEAK TO DAD!

47

MY FATHER SOUNDED EQUALLY DEFEATED.

THE DEAL I WAS WAITING FOR DIDN'T GO THROUGH. I WAS DESPERATE.

THAT'S NO EXCUSE. WHAT YOU'VE DONE IS CRIMINAL, AND WORSE—MORALLY REPREHENSIBLE. I CAN'T STAND BY AND WATCH YOU WIPE OUT MOM'S BANK ACCOUNT, OR MY FUTURE. YOU'LL BE HEARING FROM MY ATTORNEY.

ACTUALLY, THAT'S WHAT I **WISHED** I'D SAID. INSTEAD, I SIMPLY REGRESSED.

BUT I'M YOUR **DAUGHTER**. I'VE NEVER EVEN **HAD** A CREDIT CARD OF MY OWN.

MY MOTHER TOOK OUT A LOAN TO PAY OFF THE DISCOVER CARD, AND I GRADUALLY FORGAVE MY FATHER FOR WHAT I ASSUMED WAS A SINGLE TRANSGRESSION. I PROBABLY WOULDN'T HAVE FOUND OUT ABOUT THE OTHER CARDS HAD I NOT TRIED TO OPEN A BANANA REPUBLIC ACCOUNT A YEAR LATER AND GOTTEN DENIED.

CALL OUR CREDIT DEPARTMENT SO YOU CAN FIND OUT WHY YOU WERE DECLINED. MOST OF THE TIME, IT'S SOMETHING REALLY STUPID, LIKE THE INTEREST RATE ON ONE OF YOUR OTHER CREDIT CARDS WAS TOO HIGH. HERE'S THE NUMBER.

THERE'S NO OBVIOUS REASON: YOUR APPLICATION IS JUST MARKED "DECLINED." IF I WERE YOU, I'D ORDER YOUR CREDIT REPORT.

UMM... HOW DO YOU DO THAT?

THE REPORTS ARRIVED IN LESS THAN A MONTH. I COULDN'T DECIPHER THEM, SO I SHOWED THEM TO A WAITER AT THE RESTAURANT WHERE I WORKED.

LOOKS LIKE YOU OPENED A CITIBANK CARD, AN AMERICAN EXPRESS CARD, AND AN MBNA CARD.

SO I'D OPENED AND CLOSED ROUGHLY SIX CARDS, EVEN THOUGH I'D NEVER APPLIED FOR A CREDIT CARD IN MY LIFE.

I CALLED MY SISTERS AND ASKED THEM TO CHECK THEIR CREDIT REPORTS. MY FATHER HAD TAKEN OUT CARDS IN THEIR NAMES TOO.

IS DAD GOING TO GET IN TROUBLE?

I'M SURE THERE'S A GOOD REASON FOR THIS.

I ORDERED A COPY OF THE APPLICATION MY FATHER HAD SUBMITTED TO DISCOVER.

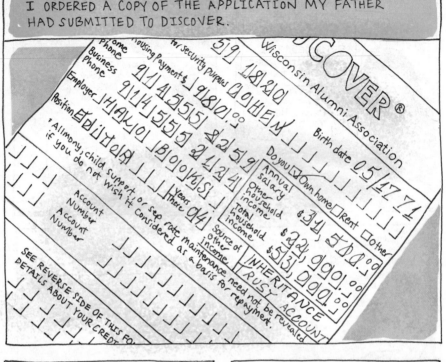

IN THE UPPER LEFT-HAND CORNER OF THE PAGE WAS A REASONABLE FACSIMILE OF MY SIGNATURE. A BIT SHAKY, PERHAPS, BUT MY SIGNATURE, NONETHELESS.

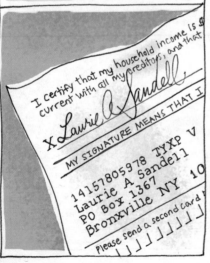

HOW DID I STAND A CHANCE AGAINST SOMEONE SO DETERMINED?

I CALLED THE SOCIAL SECURITY ADMINISTRATION TO TRY TO CHANGE MY SOCIAL SECURITY NUMBER.

IT'S POSSIBLE IF YOU FILE A FRAUD COMPLAINT AND PRESS CRIMINAL CHARGES.

I TRIED TO PICTURE MY FATHER IN AN ORANGE JUMPSUIT, SITTING ON A METAL BED, STARING AT THE FLOOR. HE WAS OVERWEIGHT. HE'D HAD THREE HEART ATTACKS AND WHEEZED WHEN HE WALKED.

I COULDN'T DO IT.

CLICK

THIS TIME, I LET MY MOTHER CONFRONT MY FATHER. AFTERWARD, SHE CALLED ME.

I'LL PAY THE OUTSTANDING BALANCES, DON'T WORRY.

TELL HIM I'VE ORDERED **CREDIT AWARE**!

I RECEIVED AN E-MAIL FROM MY FATHER.

I AM SORRY FOR THE TROUBLE AND PAIN I HAVE CAUSED YOU. THE ONLY JUSTIFICATION I CAN GIVE IS THAT IT WAS AN ACT OF DESPERATION, IN THE MIDST OF MY BUSINESS TRAVEL, WHEN I HAD TO SPEND FIRST AND PUT IN FOR EXPENSES LATER. DESPERATION HAS MADE ME DO THIS FOOLISH THING. I AM SORRY, DEEPLY SORRY! I LOVE YOU, DAD.

YEAH, **RIGHT**!

SOON AFTER THAT, MY MOTHER CALLED TO TELL ME THE BANK HAD FORECLOSED ON MY PARENTS' HOME.

I... I GUESS HE DIDN'T MAKE SOME OF THE MORTGAGE PAYMENTS.

EVENTUALLY, TIME LESSENED THE IMPACT OF WHAT MY FATHER HAD DONE UNTIL I COULDN'T REMEMBER WHY, EXACTLY, I'D BEEN SO ANGRY AT HIM.

HE HAS **NO** MONEY. AND HE CAN'T GET A JOB BECAUSE OF HIS POLITICS.

Mm HMM.

FLIGHT

THE NEXT FOUR YEARS WERE AN EXERCISE IN SELF-DESTRUCTION. I TRAVELED RELENTLESSLY. I TOLD MANY LIES. I WAS WILLING TO BE ANYTHING, TRY ANYTHING, AS LONG AS IT DIDN'T RESEMBLE THE LIFE I WAS LIVING BEFORE.

IN ISRAEL, I HAD MY FIRST AND ONLY LESBIAN FLING, WITH A YESHIVA GIRL NAMED SARAH.

FROM THE START, SHE WANTED TO BE MY GIRLFRIEND. I WANTED ONLY SEX.

I...I WORRY YOU'RE JUST EXPERIMENTING.

I'M **NOT**. I THINK YOU'RE REALLY SPECIAL.

THIS WENT ON FOR MONTHS: SARAH ATTEMPTING TO HOLD MY HAND IN PUBLIC, AND ME GIVING HER JUST ENOUGH AFFECTION TO LURE HER BACK TO MY APARTMENT AT THE END OF THE NIGHT.

YOU'RE JUST *USING ME!*

NO, I'M NOT. COME HERE.

LATER THAT NIGHT...

WHERE ARE YOU GOING?

I NEED TO WASH MY APRON FOR WORK.

BUT IT'S THREE IN THE MORNING!

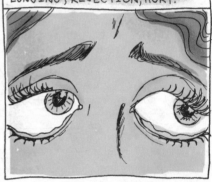

HER EYES WERE FULL OF LONGING, REJECTION, HURT.

IT'S NOT THAT I WASN'T AWARE OF WHAT I WAS DOING TO SARAH; IT'S JUST THAT THE PART OF ME THAT WANTED TO EXPERIMENT SEXUALLY WAS SPEAKING UP MORE LOUDLY THAN THE PART OF ME THAT WANTED TO BE CARING AND COMPASSIONATE.

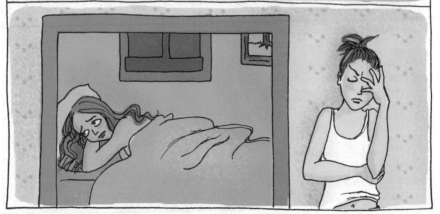

THERE WAS LAURIE, THE GOOD GIRL, WHO WON HER FATHER'S LOVE WITH CARTOONS AND AWARDS.

AND THERE WAS ANGRY, EMPATHY-FREE LAURIE, WHO REFUSED TO CATER TO ANYONE'S NEEDS BUT HER OWN.

ONE DAY, A WOMAN I WORKED WITH TOLD ME SHE'D JUST RETURNED FROM TOKYO, WHERE SHE'D WORKED AS A "HOSTESS," A SORT OF MODERN-DAY GEISHA. THE JOB INVOLVED MAKING CONVERSATION WITH JAPANESE BUSINESSMEN.

I SAVED TWENTY-FIVE THOUSAND DOLLARS.

IN *SIX MONTHS*?

TWO DAYS LATER, I SAID GOOD-BYE TO SARAH.

WHEN WERE YOU GOING TO TELL ME?

LOOK, **I** DIDN'T EVEN KNOW I WAS GOING UNTIL YESTERDAY.

I NEVER SAW SARAH—OR ANY OF THE FRIENDS I'D MADE IN ISRAEL OVER THE COURSE OF TWO YEARS—AGAIN.

WITHIN A MONTH, I WAS WORKING IN A TOKYO NIGHTCLUB CALLED THE FLAMINGO. MY NEW JOB INVOLVED FLIRTING WITH CUSTOMERS, LIGHTING THEIR CIGARETTES, AND REFILLING THEIR DRINKS. FOR THIS, I WAS PAID UPWARDS OF FOUR HUNDRED DOLLARS A NIGHT.

KONICHIWA.

THE FLAMINGO WAS ALSO A STRIP BAR. THE DANCERS, I NOTICED, MADE TRIPLE THE MONEY I MADE AND DIDN'T HAVE TO DEAL WITH CUSTOMERS.

SO KAWAII!

FIVE MONTHS INTO MY STAY IN JAPAN, I CALLED A TALENT AGENCY THAT REPRESENTED DANCERS AND SET UP AN INTERVIEW.

I TOOK A BUS TO THE OUTSKIRTS OF TOKYO. I SPENT THE RIDE NERVOUSLY REAPPLYING GLITTER TO MY EYE-LIDS AND SMOOTHING MY CRUSHED VELVET DRESS.

56

A JAMAICAN GUY MET ME AT THE BUS STOP AND TOOK ME TO A DINGY, EMPTY APARTMENT IN THE MIDDLE OF NOWHERE.

GIVE ME YOUR PASSPORT; I NEED TO PHOTOCOPY IT FOR YOUR APPLICATION.

I SURRENDERED MY PASSPORT.

YOU WAIT HERE.

NAIVE STOICISM IN THE FACE OF PERIL WAS SECOND NATURE TO ME.

YOU'RE LUCKY YOU'RE A GIRL! IF YOU WERE A BOY I WOULD KILL YOU!

WHILE I WAITED, I WATCHED A BIZARRE VIDEO CALLED SEXERCIZE. IT INVOLVED A NUDE WESTERN WOMAN LEADING A PACK OF FULLY CLOTHED JAPANESE TOURISTS AROUND A ZOO.

HERE'S YOUR PASSPORT. NOW LET'S TAKE A POLAROID SO THE CLUB OWNERS CAN GET A LOOK AT YOU.

ローリーちゃん
ストリッパー　YOKOHAMA

THE AGENCY PLACED ME AT A CLUB IN YOKOHAMA, ABOUT EIGHTEEN MILES FROM TOKYO.

THE MOVIE *STRIPTEASE* HAD JUST COME OUT IN JAPAN.

DEMI MOOORE!

DEMI MOORE!

DEMI MOOOORE!

ONCE I GOT THE HANG OF IT, I FELT POWERFUL ONSTAGE.

KONICHIWA.

AFTER MY SET, I WAS DIRECTED TO SIT WITH CUSTOMERS AND SOLICIT LAP DANCES.

LAP DANCE-U? TOUCH OK.

FOR THE FIRST TIME, I NOTICED WHAT WAS GOING ON IN DARKENED CORNERS AROUND THE ROOM.

I DEFLECTED THE DANGER WITH A POTENTLY UNSEXY BLEND OF CEREBRAL QUIPS, OBSCURE ALLUSIONS AND INTELLECTUAL REFERENCES.

UM, AS I WAS SAYING, I PLAY CLASSICAL PIANO AND SPEAK HEBREW. PHILIP ROTH IS ONE OF MY FAVORITE WRITERS...

NO ONE ASKED ME FOR A LAP DANCE.

YOU NOT COME BACK?

YOU DON'T UNDERSTAND— THIS ISN'T ME!

MEN

IN TRUTH, I HAD NO IDEA WHO I WAS. THIS WAS REFLECTED MOST GLARINGLY IN MY RELATIONSHIPS, WHERE I TENDED TO TAKE ON THE IDENTITY OF WHOMEVER I WAS WITH, UNTIL I BECAME ENRAGED WITH THAT ROLE AND RAN.

I WANT TO BREAK UP.

YOU... YOU WANT A HOT DOG?

IF I HELD ONTO ANY SENSE OF SELF AT ALL, IT WAS THE STORY I KEPT IN MY BACK POCKET — THE ONE I TOLD ABOUT MY FATHER. I USED IT TO BOND WITH MEN.

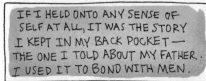

I'VE NEVER REALLY KNOWN WHAT HE DOES FOR A LIVING. MY FAMILY THINKS HE MIGHT BE IN THE C.I.A.

THAT'S INCREDIBLE.

YOU'RE INCREDIBLE.

DURING THAT PERIOD, THE MEN I DATED RANGED FROM THE CRUEL AND DISTANT TO THE WARM AND BORING TO EVERYTHING IN BETWEEN.

I TRAVELED MORE.

INDIA

JORDAN

MEXICO

FRANCE

EGYPT

THAILAND

I RETURNED TO AMERICA HAVING NO IDEA WHAT I'D LEARNED FROM MY TRAVELS AND NO CLUE WHAT I WAS GOING TO DO NEXT. MY SISTER, WHO'D GOTTEN A JOB IN FINANCE, SAID SHE COULD HELP ME FIND WORK AS A SECRETARY IN A BANK. MY FATHER HELPED ME WITH MY RESUME.

BUT IF I ADD IN ALL THOSE WAITRESSING JOBS, IT'S GOING TO BE LIKE FOUR PAGES LONG!

IT **SHOULD** BE FOUR PAGES LONG. AT **LEAST**.

I GOT THE JOB. IT WASN'T EXACTLY A DREAM JOB, BUT I'D NEVER MADE MONEY LIKE THAT BEFORE.

I STILL CALLED ON MY FATHER FOR ADVICE.

I TOOK VACATION BUT PUT IN FOR OVERTIME BY MISTAKE AND GOT AN EXTRA FIVE HUNDRED DOLLARS — I'M **FREAKING OUT!**

DON'T PANIC! JUST DON'T TELL ANYONE. FOR YEARS—**YEARS**— I DIDN'T TELL THE GOVERNMENT CERTAIN THINGS, OK?

REALLY, HE WAS THE ONLY PERSON WHO UNDERSTOOD.

63

ONE NIGHT, I HAD DINNER WITH MY HIGH-SCHOOL FRIEND, JENNY, AND HER HUSBAND, ANDY, WHO WAS AN EDITOR AT A PRESTIGIOUS MEN'S MAGAZINE.

I STARTED TO TELL THEM STORIES ABOUT MY FATHER.

DID I EVER TELL YOU GUYS ABOUT THE TIME HE SMUGGLED KNIVES ON A FLIGHT OUT OF GERMANY?

YOU'VE GOTTA WRITE THIS SHIT **DOWN**. YOU COULD PUBLISH THIS.

THE NEXT TIME I SAW MY FATHER, I ASKED HIM HOW HE FELT ABOUT LETTING ME INTERVIEW HIM FOR A MAGAZINE ARTICLE

I'M SIXTY-THREE YEARS OF AGE NOW.... QUITE FRANKLY, WHAT'S GONNA HAPPEN? I NO LONGER PLAN TO RUN FOR POLITICAL OFFICE.

WHEN MY FATHER ARRIVED THE FOLLOWING WEEK, HE WAS TEN MINUTES EARLY, AS ALWAYS.

WHERE ARE THE EMTs?

I TOOK HIS COAT FROM HIM, A
GREEN BARN JACKET DECORATED
WITH A CONSTELLATION OF PINS
AND MEDALS: AN AMERICAN FLAG,
A PURPLE HEART, THE SKULL
AND CROSSBONES OF THE
SPECIAL FORCES.

HE SETTLED INTO A STIFF-
BACKED CHAIR AND I SAT
ACROSS FROM HIM ON THE
COUCH. HE STARTED TO TALK.

TAPE
RECORDER

IN NINETEEN SEVENTY-THREE, WHEN I WAS A PROFESSOR AT STANFORD,
THE NIXON ADMINISTRATION OFFERED ME THE
POSITION OF DEPUTY ASSISTANT SECRETARY OF STATE
FOR INTER-AMERICAN AFFAIRS. SOMEHOW A
SITUATION CAME ABOUT THAT I SPENT TWO AND
A HALF HOURS WITH HENRY KISSINGER
IN HIS OFFICE AT THE STATE DEPARTMENT.
HE HAD QUITE A REPUTATION AS A
LADIES' MAN BEFORE HE GOT MARRIED.
WHY? **WOMEN LIKE POWER!** ANYWAY,
HE WAS VERY NICE TO ME, VERY
FRIENDLY, SO MUCH SO THAT SIXTEEN
YEARS LATER, I BECAME A
CONSULTANT TO THE NATIONAL
SECURITY COUNCIL...

THAT FIRST NIGHT, HE SPOKE FOR HOURS—I JUST
LISTENED. IN NO TIME, I WAS UTTERLY
ENTRANCED BY MY FATHER'S STORIES.

65

HE'D RUBBED SHOULDERS WITH A FUTURE JUSTICE OF THE U.S. SUPREME COURT.

"ANTHONY KENNEDY AND I WERE COLLEAGUES AT THE UNIVERSITY OF THE PACIFIC. OH, WE USED TO TALK FOR **HOURS** IN THE FACULTY ROOM."

PARACHUTED INTO THE VIETNAMESE JUNGLE WITH GENERAL WESTMORELAND.

"THE GENERAL PLUMMETED OUT OF THE TREE, AND THAT'S HOW I BECAME KNOWN AS THE MAN WHO DROPPED WESTMORELAND!"

OH, **SHIT**!

BECOME PEN PALS WITH POPE JOHN PAUL II.

"I STARTED CORRESPONDING WITH A YOUNG POLISH MONSIGNOR WHO WAS A PROFESSOR AT THE PONTIFICAL COLLEGE IN ROME. HIS NAME WAS KAROL WOJTYLA."

IT WAS NEARING MIDNIGHT WHEN WE STOPPED.

WELL, I THINK THAT'S ENOUGH FOR TONIGHT.

WE STARTED TO MEET ON A WEEKLY BASIS. HE TOLD ME ABOUT VIETNAM...

"ALL OF A SUDDEN, SOMEBODY YELLS, '**GRENADE**!' IN MY PANIC— IN MY **PROFOUND** PANIC — I STOOD UP, GRABBED MY HELMET OFF, AND THAT THING CAME, AND I TURNED AND CAUGHT IT IN THE AIR AND THREW IT BACK, WITH MY HELMET AND EVERYTHING. ALL OF A SUDDEN, '**BOOM**!' IT CAME AT ME, AND I LUNGED— I DON'T KNOW HOW; DON'T ASK ME TO REPEAT IT. IT WAS CARNAGE LIKE NOTHING ELSE."

AND THE BUSINESS HE WAS TRYING TO ESTABLISH...

"WHO ARE THE PROSPECTIVE BUYERS OF A TECHNOLOGY LIKE THIS ONE? PEOPLE LIKE BILL GATES, MICHAEL DELL — IN OTHER WORDS, I'M GOING TO CONTACT THE THOUSAND RICHEST MEN IN THE WORLD. BECAUSE I'VE ALREADY ESTABLISHED A LAW: I WILL NOT WORK FOR **ANYBODY** UNLESS THE MONEY IS UP FRONT. MONEY TALKS, BULLSHIT WALKS. PERIOD. AT SIXTY-THREE, IF I HAVEN'T LEARNED THAT, I'M IN REAL TROUBLE."

AND A DUEL HE'D BEEN IN, IN ARGENTINA.

"WAS MY HEART POUNDING? WHAT DO YOU MEAN, WAS IT POUNDING? IT WAS JUMPING OUT OF MY EARS! DO YOU REALIZE WHAT YOU'RE DOING HERE? YOU'RE GOING TO SHOOT AT A MAN, AND HE'S GOING TO SHOOT AT YOU, AND YOU'RE GOING TO BE DEAD!"

SOON, HE WAS DRIVING INTO THE CITY ON A WEEKLY BASIS TO MEET WITH ME. HIS STORIES, THEY WERE BECOMING AN ADDICTION.

WHO WAS THE GUY WHO HAD THE CLEANEST CLOSET? ME. WHO WAS THE GUY WHO HAD THE NEATEST LOCKER? ME. WHO WAS THE GUY WHO HAD THE BEST-PRESSED CLOTHES AND THE SMARTEST SALUTE? ME. AND DON'T THINK FOR A MOMENT THAT THE COMPANY COMMANDER DIDN'T NOTICE.

DURING THESE CONVERSATIONS, I IGNORED THE PHONE. I DIDN'T HEAR MY ROOMMATE COME IN. I FELT CLOSER TO MY FATHER THAN I HAD IN YEARS.

DID I BELIEVE HIM? HALF OF ME DID.

THE OTHER HALF **WANTED** TO BELIEVE HIM BUT HAD SERIOUS RESERVATIONS.

I SPENT ALL DAY, EVERY DAY, AT MY SECRETARIAL JOB, TRANS-CRIBING INTERVIEWS.

AT NIGHT, I WOULD LIE IN BED, READING AND RE-READING THE TRANSCRIPTS.

STAYING UP LATE TO READ TRANSCRIPTS, THEN GETTING UP EARLY FOR WORK TOOK ITS TOLL—I STARTED TO HAVE TERRIBLE INSOMNIA.

I MENTIONED THE DIFFICULTY I WAS HAVING TO MY MOTHER — I KNEW SHE SUFFERED FROM INSOMNIA, TOO.

HAVE YOU EVER TRIED AMBIEN?

SHE SENT ME A HANDFUL OF PILLS AND TOLD ME TO BREAK THEM IN HALF.

I WAITED UNTIL SUNDAY TO TAKE ONE — THE NIGHT I TENDED TO HAVE THE MOST TROUBLE FALLING ASLEEP.

WITHIN MINUTES, I WAS OUT COLD, IN THE KIND OF DEEP, DREAMY SLUMBER I HADN'T EXPERIENCED SINCE CHILDHOOD.

THE NEXT MORNING I WOKE UP REFRESHED. WITHIN THREE WEEKS, I WAS TAKING IT EVERY NIGHT, MY SLEEP TROUBLES OVER.

EVERY SO OFTEN, ANDY, WHO WAS NOW MY EDITOR, WOULD CHECK IN, AND I'D TELL HIM THE LATEST STORY.

HE TOLD YOU WHAT? YOU DON'T BELIEVE HIM, DO YOU? THOSE STORIES ARE INSANE!

THE TALES HE TOLD **WERE** INSANE AND YET...

"OUR SECOND-IN-COMMANDS CHECKED OUR PISTOLS TO MAKE SURE THAT THEY WERE LOADED, AND WE STOOD BACK-TO-BACK."

READING THE TRANSCRIPTS IN ORDER, ABSORBING THE STORIES AS A WHOLE...

"THERE WAS ONE THING THEY DIDN'T COUNT ON: THIS YOUNG KID, THIS YOUNG PUP THAT THEY WERE DEFYING, WAS A CRACK SHOT. THEY DIDN'T KNOW THAT. **I** KNEW THAT."

I SECRETLY BELIEVED THERE WAS A POSSIBILITY HE WAS TELLING THE TRUTH.

"THEN THEY SAY, **FUEGO!** FIRE! HIS BULLET PASSED ME LIKE THIS. I'M NOT KIDDING YOU, SWEETIE. I **FELT** IT. NO QUESTION. MINE, UNFORTUNATELY, LANDED RIGHT HERE, BETWEEN THE EYES. I KILLED HIM. BELIEVE ME, A BULLET GOES RIGHT THROUGH."

71

AFTER ALL, I'D **SEEN** MY FATHER PERFORM ASTOUNDING FEATS WITH MY OWN EYES.

WANT TO TRY IT?

OF COURSE, I WAS A CHILD THEN, AND NOT TRAINED TO LOOK FOR INCONSISTENCIES.

THE LIEUTENANT COMMANDER SAID, "TAKE YOUR BERET OFF." THEN HE HANDED ME A GREEN BERET WITH THE SPECIAL FORCES LOGO ON IT. I LOOKED AT IT, TOTALLY SHOCKED, AND SAID, "BUT I DIDN'T GO THROUGH TRAINING..." HE SAID, "DON'T YOU WORRY, SON. IF YOU SURVIVE THE NEXT SIX MONTHS HERE, YOU WILL HAVE EARNED IT."

THE INTERVIEWS CONTINUED. EVENTUALLY, I HAD MORE THAN THREE HUNDRED PAGES TRANSCRIBED. ANDY KEPT CALLING TO SEE IF I'D FACT-CHECKED MY FATHER'S CLAIMS.

WHAT ARE YOU WAITING FOR? CALL THE UNIVERSITIES.

HE STILL HASN'T TOLD ME ABOUT LANGUAGE SCHOOL, AND I DON'T WANT TO INTERRUPT OUR GROOVE.

REALLY, I JUST DIDN'T **WANT** TO KNOW. THE STORIES KEPT OUR RELATIONSHIP INTACT. TO BE HONEST, THEY WERE KEEPING **ME** INTACT.

ONE DAY, I OPENED UP MY OLD HOTMAIL ACCOUNT, WHICH I HADN'T USED IN AGES, AND FOUND AN E-MAIL FROM MY FATHER. IT WAS JUST A FEW DAYS OLD.

ONE QUICK GLANCE AND I KNEW IT WASN'T INTENDED FOR ME. IT SEEMED HE HAD CC'D ME BY MISTAKE.

TO: MAIFENG @ HOTMAIL.COM
MY BELOVED MAI,
AFTER OUR CONVERSATION LAST NIGHT, I FELT TERRIBLY SAD. AFTER SIXTY-THREE YEARS OF SUCCESS, HAVING BECOME FAMOUS, HAVING ACCOMPLISHED EVERYTHING I HAD SET OUT TO DO, I FIND MYSELF NOW TO BE A LOSER, AND AM NOT SURE I CAN HANDLE ALL THESE REVERSES AT THE SAME TIME. THE FEELING THAT YOU WERE WITH ME IS THE ONLY THING THAT HAS SUSTAINED ME ALL THESE MONTHS. REGARDLESS OF THE SITUATION, I WILL HELP YOU ANYWAY. UNFORTUNATELY, I DON'T HAVE THE WEALTH THAT I ONCE HAD, OTHERWISE I WOULD HELP YOU A LOT MORE. I LOVE YOU AND ALWAYS WILL.

I CALLED KARYN.

ARE YOU KIDDING? READ IT TO ME AGAIN.

I DID.

HE SOUNDS SUICIDAL. **OH MY GOD**—WHAT IF HE'S KILLING HIMSELF **RIGHT NOW**?

I'M CALLING DAD.

HELLO?

ANY AFTERNOON PLANS?

MOMMY AND I ARE GOING TO CHECK OUT THE GOYA EXHIBIT.

THAT SOUNDS LIKE FUN.

OH, I'M SURE IT'LL BE MAGNIFICENT.

CLEARLY, HE HAD NO IDEA HE'D SENT ME THIS E-MAIL—NOR WAS HE IN THE MIDDLE OF KILLING HIMSELF.

THESE PAST TWO YEARS, WE'D GROWN AS CLOSE AS I'D EVER IMAGINED WE COULD POSSIBLY BE. I'D BEEN SUCKED INTO TRUSTING HIM **AGAIN**. I WAS ANGRIER AT MYSELF THAN I WAS AT HIM.

AS SOON AS I HUNG UP, I MADE THREE CALLS: TO COLUMBIA UNIVERSITY, WHERE MY FATHER GOT HIS PHD ; TO NYU, WHERE HE GOT HIS JD, AND TO STANFORD UNIVERSITY, WHERE HE TAUGHT ECONOMICS.

NONE OF THEM HAD EVER HEARD OF HIM.

I CALLED THE COMMUNITY COLLEGE WHERE MY FATHER HAD WORKED FROM 1981 TO 1983. I MANAGED TO TRACK DOWN THE DEAN WHO HAD HIRED HIM.

I REMEMBER YOUR FATHER WELL—HE WAS ONE OF THE BEST TEACHERS WE EVER HAD. BUT THEN HE CHANGED. HE BECAME AGGRESSIVE WITH COLLEAGUES, ALMOST BIPOLAR.

AT THE END OF THE SEMESTER, HE TURNED IN A STACK OF STUDENT EVALUATIONS, EVERY SINGLE ONE OF THEM MARKED "EXCELLENT"— ALL IN THE SAME PEN, SAME HANDWRITING.

I DID MY OWN BACKGROUND CHECK AND FOUND OUT THAT HE'D BEEN IMPERSONATING A HARVARD PROFESSOR. WHEN I CONFRONTED HIM, HE HANDED IN HIS RESIGNATION AND LEFT WITHOUT SAYING GOOD-BYE. I HEARD HE WAS TEACHING AT RAMAPO COLLEGE AFTER THAT.

DID YOU WARN THE ADMINISTRATION THERE?

NO. I LIKED YOUR FATHER VERY MUCH.

I SENT AWAY FOR MY FATHER'S MILITARY RECORDS AND RECEIVED A TWO-PAGE DOCUMENT FROM THE NATIONAL PERSONNEL RECORDS CENTER. HIS RANK WAS LISTED AS PRIVATE. NO PURPLE HEARTS OR BRONZE STARS. NO MENTION OF HIS EVER HAVING SET FOOT IN VIETNAM.

I CALLED MY MOTHER TO SEE WHAT SHE HAD TO SAY. TO MY SURPRISE, SHE DIDN'T EXACTLY DENY THE CHARGES.

BUT HE *TOLD* ME HE HAD THOSE DEGREES.

WHAT DO YOU MEAN, HE 'TOLD' YOU? DID YOU SEE HIM STUDYING? MEET HIS GRAD SCHOOL BUDDIES?

STOP BOMBARDING ME WITH QUESTIONS — I CAN HARDLY THINK.

AN HOUR LATER, MY PHONE RANG AGAIN. IT WAS MY MOTHER, SPEAKING IN A VOICE THAT SOUNDED ALMOST ROBOTIC.

THERE ARE REASONS, SOMETIMES, WHY PEOPLE'S NAMES AREN'T IN THE PUBLIC EYE.

WHAT? IS DAD TELLING YOU TO SAY THAT?

I HAVE TO GO.

I RECOGNIZED MY MOTHER'S BLIND FAITH IN MY FATHER.

DIAL TONE

IT LOOKED LIKE THE FAITH *I* ONCE HAD.

THIS EXQUISITE SET OF ROSARY BEADS WAS GIVEN TO MY FATHER BY THE POPE HIMSELF.

IN THAT MOMENT, ANY RESERVATIONS I HAD ABOUT WRITING ABOUT MY FATHER EVAPORATED. I CALLED UP MY SISTERS AND MY EDITOR, ANDY, TO TELL THEM WHAT I PLANNED TO DO.

YOU'RE GOING TO *PUBLISH* THIS?

BUT WHAT ABOUT MOM?

ARE YOU SURE YOU'RE READY TO DO THIS? EXPOSE YOUR FATHER AS A FRAUD IN FRONT OF THE WHOLE WORLD?

RELATIVE IMPOSTOR

ONE WEEK LATER, I ASKED MY FATHER TO MEET ME AT STARBUCKS.

WHAT'S THAT FOR?

I'M OLD, HIJA, WHAT CAN I TELL YOU?

SO, I DON'T KNOW HOW MUCH MOM TOLD YOU—

IF YOU EVER HAVE SOMETHING TO TELL ME, THE **LAST** PERSON I WANT YOU TO TALK TO IS MY WIFE.

SLAM.

DAD, I CHECKED WITH SOME OF THE UNIVERSITIES YOU SAY YOU WENT TO, AND, UM, THEY'VE NEVER HEARD OF YOU.

YOU ARE WALKING INTO A MINEFIELD.

I DON'T CARE IF YOU'VE KILLED PEOPLE. I DON'T CARE IF YOU'RE RUNNING A BABY-SMUGGLING RING. YOU CAN TELL ME.

THAT'S GOOD TO KNOW. BUT IT'S TOO LATE. I'M IN TOO DEEP.

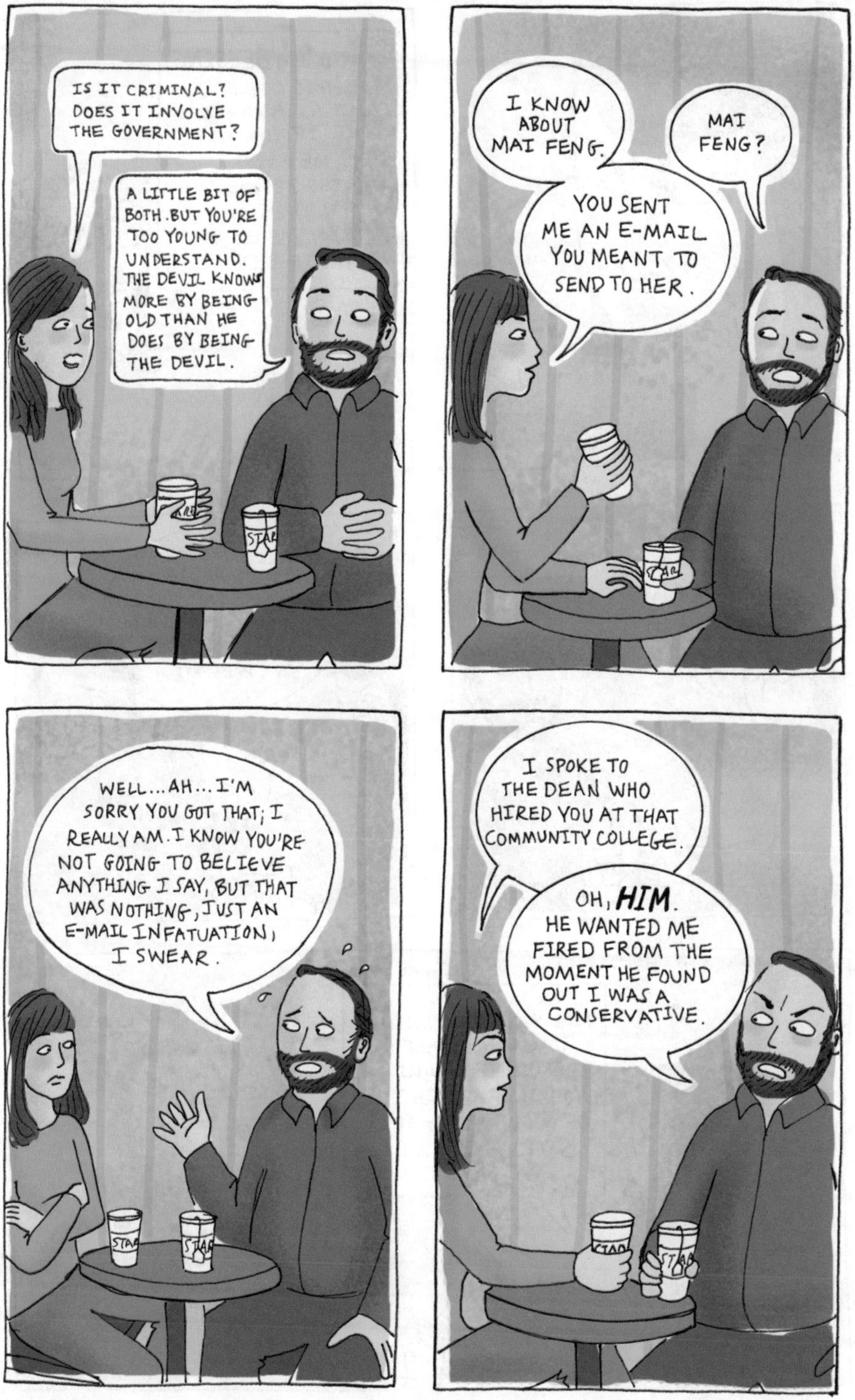
IS IT CRIMINAL? DOES IT INVOLVE THE GOVERNMENT?
A LITTLE BIT OF BOTH. BUT YOU'RE TOO YOUNG TO UNDERSTAND. THE DEVIL KNOWS MORE BY BEING OLD THAN HE DOES BY BEING THE DEVIL.
I KNOW ABOUT MAI FENG.
MAI FENG?
YOU SENT ME AN E-MAIL YOU MEANT TO SEND TO HER.
WELL... AH... I'M SORRY YOU GOT THAT; I REALLY AM. I KNOW YOU'RE NOT GOING TO BELIEVE ANYTHING I SAY, BUT THAT WAS NOTHING, JUST AN E-MAIL INFATUATION, I SWEAR.
I SPOKE TO THE DEAN WHO HIRED YOU AT THAT COMMUNITY COLLEGE.
OH, **HIM**. HE WANTED ME FIRED FROM THE MOMENT HE FOUND OUT I WAS A CONSERVATIVE.

LAURIE, I'M **BEGGING** YOU. THIS COULDN'T COME AT A WORSE TIME. IF YOU JUST GIVE ME A FEW MONTHS BEFORE YOU WRITE THE STORY... I'M ON THE EDGE OF A BIG DEAL.

A DEAL, HUH?

WRITE THE STORY. WRITE IT—AND LET THE CARDS FALL WHERE THEY MAY. IF I CAN'T HANDLE IT WHEN IT COMES OUT...

I WON'T.

ARE YOU THREATENING TO KILL YOURSELF? BECAUSE IF YOU KILL YOURSELF AS A RESULT OF MY WRITING THIS STORY, IT'S NOT MY FAULT.

80

IT'S GETTING LATE. I HAVE TO FEED THE METER.

DO YOU UNDERSTAND? **NOT MY FAULT**!

I DON'T KNOW WHAT I EXPECTED — CATHARSIS? A SENSE OF CLOSURE? I FELT NOTHING BUT A BITTER EMPTINESS.

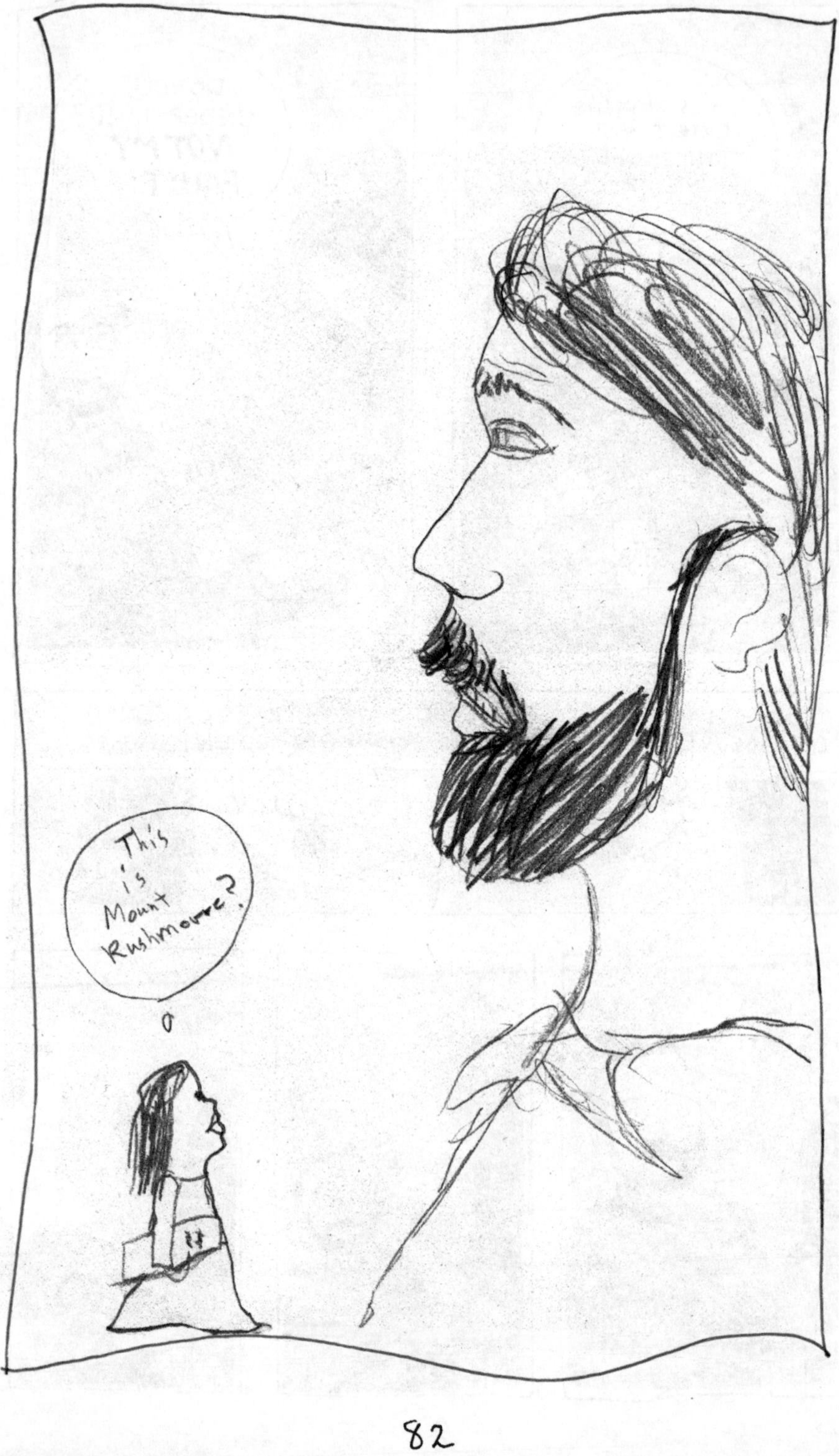
This is Mount Rushmoore?

FATHER FICTION

I LEFT THE BANK TO BECOME A FREELANCE WRITER. MY FATHER AND I DIDN'T SPEAK WHILE I WORKED ON THE STORY.

YOU KNOW, DADDY CAME INTO THE CITY SO MANY TIMES TO TALK TO YOU.

I KNOW.

WELL, HE'S NOT GOING TO TALK TO YOU ANYMORE. I'M NOT SURE HE'S *EVER* GOING TO TALK TO YOU AGAIN.

I KNOW.

AND WHAT AM I SUPPOSED TO TELL PEOPLE — THAT YOU'RE WRITING A TELL-ALL ABOUT US?

TELL THEM WHATEVER YOU WANT.

THE TEACHERS AT SCHOOL TALK. MY COUSINS TALK.

I CAN'T WORRY ABOUT WHAT PEOPLE SAY ANYMORE.

MY BIRTHDAY WENT BY WITHOUT A PHONE CALL FROM MY FATHER, SO I KNEW HE MEANT BUSINESS. MOTHER'S DAY, FATHER'S DAY, AND MY MOTHER'S BIRTHDAY ALL PASSED. MY PARENTS AND SISTERS MET UP FOR HOLIDAYS WITHOUT ME.

MY SISTERS WERE SUPPORTIVE OF ME, BUT NOT OF THE STORY I WAS WRITING.

OK, SO HE WASN'T IN VIETNAM. BUT DO YOU HAVE TO PUBLICLY HUMILIATE HIM?

CAN'T YOU JUST SEE A SHRINK?

I DID FEEL GUILTY. HADN'T HE WRITTEN A BAY OF PIGS PAPER FOR ME IN THE SEVENTH GRADE? AND THIS WAS HOW I REPAID HIM...

OTHER TIMES, ANGER ECLIPSED MY GUILT. HE'D LIED TO ME AS A KID! AS A TEEN! AS A *JOURNALIST*!

FOR THE MOMENT, I IGNORED MY DILEMMA AND SPENT ALL MY TIME WRITING AT THE NEW YORK PUBLIC LIBRARY. SEEING MY FATHER'S CRIMES LAID OUT ON-SCREEN DIDN'T MAKE THE ACT OF EXPOSING HIM EASIER; IF ANYTHING, *I* FELT EXPOSED. I WAS THE MONSTER MY FATHER HAD ALWAYS ACCUSED ME OF BEING, THE BAD SEED. IF MY FATHER DIED OF A HEART ATTACK AFTER HE READ IT, I'D BE RESPONSIBLE. IT WAS AN UNDERLYING FEAR I'D HAD SINCE I WAS TWELVE YEARS OLD — SOMEHOW, IN SOME WAY, I'D BE RESPONSIBLE FOR HIS DEMISE. AND YET...

I KNEW I WASN'T GOING TO BE FREE OF HIM UNTIL I UNDERSTOOD HIM. HE'D IMPLICATED ME IN HIS CRIMES, MAKING THEM MY CRIMES. HIS STORY WAS MY STORY TOO.

TWO WEEKS BEFORE I HANDED IN MY FINAL DRAFT, I GOT A STRANGE PHONE CALL.

A PRIVATE INVESTIGATOR?! AM I IN SOME KIND OF TROUBLE?

THE MAN'S NAME WAS AL MCEVOY. HE WAS REPRESENTING A MAN NAMED JORGE LOPEZ.

IN SEPTEMBER, YOUR FATHER WENT TO CHINA TO SELL SOME TECHNOLOGY ON MY CLIENT'S BEHALF. HE HASN'T HEARD FROM HIM SINCE. IS YOUR FATHER STILL IN THE COUNTRY?

I HAVE NO IDEA. WE'RE NOT... IN TOUCH.

WOULD YOU BE WILLING TO TALK TO MR. LOPEZ? SAYS HE'S A FRIEND. HE JUST WANTS TO MAKE SURE YOUR FATHER IS OK.

DO YOU WANT TO GIVE ME HIS NUMBER?

ACTUALLY, HE'LL CALL YOU, AT NOON. HE'S IN A HOTEL IN MANHATTAN.

12:00 P.M. SHARP

CLICK

FIRST, I MUST APOLOGIZE: I AM TERRIBLY SORRY TO DISTURB YOU. IT'S JUST THAT MY WIFE AND I HAVE NOT HEARD FROM YOUR FATHER AND ARE WORRIED ABOUT HIM.

86

SO YOU'RE A FRIEND OF HIS?

A FRIEND AND BUSINESS PARTNER. ABOUT A YEAR AGO, MY WIFE AND I SENT HIM ON A TRIP TO CHINA TO SELL SOME TECHNOLOGY WE'D INVENTED...

HE WAS GOING TO SELL IT TO THE WORLD'S THOUSAND RICHEST MEN?

YES, THAT'S IT! AND WE HAVEN'T HEARD FROM HIM SINCE. I'VE SENT LETTERS, MANY E-MAILS, AND LEFT PHONE MESSAGES. BUT HE HASN'T RESPONDED TO ANY OF THEM.

WHO IS THIS PRIVATE INVESTIGATOR WHO CALLED ME?

WELL, WHEN I VISITED THE POLICE STATION IN BRONXVILLE...

THE *POLICE*?

YES, WHEN YOUR FATHER DIDN'T RESPOND TO ANY OF MY LETTERS I FLEW TO NEW YORK TO CHECK ON MY INVESTMENT.

AND WHAT IS IT YOU WANT FROM MY FATHER?

I WOULD LIKE TO RECEIVE THE MATERIALS HE HAS PROMISED TO DELIVER AND RECEIPTS FOR THE MONEY WE'VE SENT.

HOW MUCH HAVE YOU PAID HIM ALREADY?

I SEE. SO A TOTAL OF THREE HUNDRED AND FORTY THOUSAND DOLLARS.

I TOOK HIS INFORMATION AND GOT OFF THE PHONE. MY HEART HURT FOR THIS MAN. I KNEW HE WOULD NEVER SEE HIS MONEY AGAIN.

MY ARTICLE ON MY FATHER APPEARED IN APRIL. I DIDN'T PUT MY NAME ON IT.

GUIDE TO DRINK

MY FATHER, THE FRAUD BY ANONYMOUS

HE SAID, "I'M IN TOO DEEP."

EACH OF MY FAMILY MEMBERS REACTED TO IT IN THEIR OWN WAY.

OH, **THAT**— WELL, I'M NOT PLANNING TO READ IT.

SO IS IT OUT OF YOUR SYSTEM NOW?

BARNEY'S

WHY DIDN'T YOU TELL ME ABOUT THE LETTER? I WANT TO KNOW MORE... WAIT, DON'T TELL ME. I FEEL TOO GUILTY.

DID MY FATHER READ THE STORY? TO THIS DAY, I DON'T KNOW. BY THE TIME IT CAME OUT, WE HADN'T SPOKEN IN MORE THAN A YEAR. AS FOR ME, I THOUGHT IT WOULD PROVIDE THE KIND OF CATHARSIS I'D BEEN LOOKING FOR, BUT I FELT MORE UNMOORED THAN EVER. NOTHING HAD CHANGED: MY FAMILY CONTINUED TO BE INSISTENTLY BLIND TO THE TRUTH. I REMAINED THE LONE VOICE OF PROTEST. THE PIECE SAT ANONYMOUSLY ON NEWSSTANDS, THEN JUST AS QUIETLY DISAPPEARED.

89

Part II

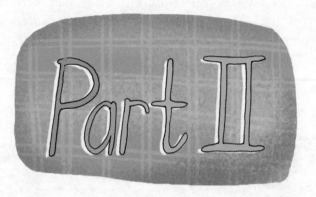

STARSTRUCK

SOON AFTER, I LANDED A JOB AT A POPULAR WOMEN'S MAGAZINE.

MY MOTHER BRAGGED ABOUT MY NEW JOB TO ALL HER FRIENDS. MAINLY, SHE WAS RELIEVED I'D WRITTEN THE STORY ABOUT MY DAD ANONYMOUSLY.

EVERYONE WAS SO IMPRESSED WHEN THEY HEARD YOU'RE GOING TO BE ON STAFF!

ONE DAY, MY EDITOR WAS IN A PANIC. THE WRITER FOR OUR SEPTEMBER COVER STORY ON PENÉLOPE CRUZ HAD FALLEN THROUGH. SHE ASKED IF I WOULD LIKE TO DO A LAST-MINUTE INTERVIEW WITH THE SPANISH STAR.

WHAT DO YOU THINK?

WOULD I **LIKE** TO? I WAS **THRILLED**!

CELEBRITY TRIVIA WAS A SECRET HOBBY OF MINE. I READ TABLOIDS BY THE BUSHEL. I ACTUALLY KNEW PENELOPE WAS VACATIONING WITH MATTHEW MCCONAUGHEY AT A RESORT SOMEWHERE IN LOUISIANA.

HERE'S WHERE THEY'RE STAYING.

MAPQUEST

THE INTERVIEW WENT OFF WITHOUT A HITCH.

THIS EES PENELOPE.

THANK YOU—THAT EES VERY SWEET!

OH, TOM* AND I ARE STILL GREAT FRIENDS.

*CRUISE

EM, I WOULD SAY PEDRO ALMODÓVAR.

I AM MORE PROUD OF THEES FILM THAN ANY OTHER.

CIAO!

92

NEXT THING I KNEW, I WAS FLYING TO LOS ANGELES TO INTERVIEW CARMEN ELECTRA.

HERE'S WHY THIS IS AN IMPORTANT ASSIGNMENT. SHE'S GOING TO TALK ABOUT THE DEATHS OF HER MOTHER AND SISTER.

AND STAYING AT THE FOUR SEASONS IN BEVERLY HILLS.

I'D FORGOTTEN HOW MUCH I HATED TO FLY.

THEN I REMEMBERED THE AMBIEN IN MY BAG. I'D BEEN TAKING IT EVERY NIGHT TO SLEEP — WHY NOT TO FLY?

I POPPED A PILL. FIFTEEN MINUTES LATER, MY FEAR HAD MELTED AWAY ENTIRELY. I WOKE UP WHEN WE TOUCHED DOWN ON THE TARMAC.

MISS, WE'RE HERE.

I WAS STILL GROGGY WHEN I CHECKED IN, SO I TOOK A LONG, LUXURIOUS NAP IN MY KING-SIZE BED. I WOKE UP REFRESHED AND **THRILLED** WITH MY SURROUNDINGS.

THAT NIGHT, I HAD DINNER WITH A GIRLFRIEND OF MINE WHO LIVED IN L.A.

WHEN YOU DROP ME OFF, CAN YOU SHOW ME HOW TO USE THAT NERVE-DOT-COM SERVICE?

I'M TELLING YOU, IT'S THE GREATEST. LIKE SHOPPING THROUGH AN ONLINE CATALOGUE OF MEN.

I'D GOTTEN A FEW BOYFRIENDS OUT OF THE INTERNET DATING THING AND THOUGHT SHE OUGHT TO TRY IT. THAT'S WHEN I STUMBLED ACROSS BEN'S PROFILE.

OOH, HE'S CUTE—MIND IF I TAKE THIS ONE FOR MYSELF?

BEN WAS A SCREENWRITER WHO HAD GREAT TASTE IN BOOKS.

THE PHOTO HE'D POSTED WAS A SIMPLE ONE, A SELF-PORTRAIT IN FRONT OF A WHITE WALL.

BEN310 HAS 1 photo
Upgrade to see full-size photos

nerve   HOME | PERSON

MY ACCOUNT   SEARCH   BROWS

BEN 310   SILVER

"I'M A GENIUS AND NOBODY KNOWS IT BUT ME."

BUKOWSKI QUOTE

ADD TO FAVORITE PHOTOS   ◀▶

BEN310 has 1 photo
Upgrade to see full-size photos

Interact with BEN310

☑ Send an email   ☺ Flirt
⊘ Block emails/winks   ⇨ Refer to a friend
▤ Add to Hotlist   ⋔ Invite to Network

31-year-old Man in Los Angeles, CA

Me

Height:	6 ft. 1 in
Body Type:	Athletic
Hair Color:	Brown
Eye Color:	Blue
Last visit:	Today
Occupation:	Screenwriter
Education:	College
Ethnicity:	Caucasian
Speaks:	English
Religion:	Agnostic
Cigarettes:	I'm a nonsmoker
Booze:	I'm a light/social drinker
Drugs:	I don't use drugs

HIS PROFILE STOOD OUT BECAUSE HE SEEMED SO HUMBLE. HIS WRITING WAS CLEAR AND STRAIGHTFORWARD – THE PERSON I IMAGINED *HE* WAS.

HERE GOES NOTHING.

CLICK!

95

THE NEXT DAY, I HEADED OVER TO THE BEVERLY HILLS HOTEL TO INTERVIEW CARMEN ELECTRA.

MADAME, THIS WAS MARILYN MONROE'S FAVORITE BUNGALOW. WOULD YOU LIKE ME TO LIGHT A FIRE?

I'D BEEN ALLOWED TO RENT IT FOR A FEW HOURS SO WE COULD HAVE A PRIVATE CONVERSATION. IT WAS SO **BEAUTIFUL.**

IT WAS STRANGE, ALMOST IRONIC TO HAVE BEEN USHERED INTO A PLACE LIKE THIS. MY FATHER HAD WHEEDLED AND SCHEMED TO ACHIEVE FAR LESS.

RIGHT OVER HERE IS FINE.

TWENTY MINUTES LATER, MY CELL PHONE RANG.

CARMEN HURT HER FOOT DANCING WITH THE PUSSYCAT DOLLS. CAN YOU COME TO HER HOUSE INSTEAD?

I RAN TO THE FRONT DESK TO SEE IF I COULD CANCEL THE ROOM.

SORRY, THERE'S NOTHING WE CAN DO. WE'LL HAVE TO CHARGE YOU FOR THE BREAKFAST TOO.

OK, CAN YOU PUT IT ON MY CORPORATE CARD?

RUMMAGE RUMMAGE

WHEN I ENTERED THE HOUSE, I FOUND IT VIRTUALLY UNFURNISHED SAVE FOR A WHITE COUCH, A BLACK GRAND PIANO, AND AN AIRBRUSHED PAINTING OF CARMEN ELECTRA'S FACE THAT TOOK UP AN ENTIRE WALL.

WE SETTLED IN ON THE COUCH. AS SOON AS I STARTED TO ASK QUESTIONS, MY NERVOUSNESS WENT AWAY. FIGURING OUT WHAT A PERSON WANTED TO TALK ABOUT, BECOMING ABSORBED IN THEIR STORIES — THAT WAS MY SPECIALTY.

WHEN YOU ARRIVED AT YOUR SISTER'S HOUSE, WHAT DID YOU SEE?

THE TREES... THE HOUSE... EVERYTHING THAT WAS BEAUTIFUL WAS DEAD.

TAPE RECORDER

I FLEW BACK TO NEW YORK, WROTE THE STORY, AND WAS TOLD IT HAD MOVED MY EDITOR TO TEARS.

AMERICAN

IT LOOKED, AT LAST, LIKE I'D FOUND MY CALLING.

STARS!

I HAD A GIFT FOR CONNECTING WITH CELEBRITIES.

"CARMEN, I KNOW EXACTLY WHAT YOU'RE TALKING ABOUT."
"YOU DO?"
"I DO."

AND I DID.

98

MOST OF THEM LIVED IN EMOTIONAL CASTLES SURROUNDED BY MOATS, AND I'D BEEN BUILDING A TOWER AROUND MYSELF FOR THIRTY-TWO YEARS.

LIKE THE WOMEN I INTERVIEWED, I'D PERFECTED THE ART OF SEEMING INCREDIBLY OPEN, WITHOUT GIVING TOO MUCH OF MYSELF AWAY.

AND I KNEW JUST HOW TO VALIDATE WHATEVER IDENTITY THEY WANTED TO CREATE.

I'M JUST NOT THAT PARTY GIRL ANYMORE.

I CAN SEE THAT.

IT WAS A SKILL THAT COULDN'T BE FAKED — ONE I'D BEEN CULTIVATING ALL MY LIFE.

TELL THE GRENADE STORY!

WELL, OK...

TWO DAYS AFTER MY INTERVIEW, I RETURNED TO NEW YORK. THERE WAS AN E-MAIL WAITING FOR ME FROM BEN.

HI LAURIE,
YOU SOUND SO INTERESTING. TOO BAD YOU LIVE IN BROOKLYN. I WAS INTRIGUED BY YOUR BOOK CHOICES BECAUSE I'VE READ AND ENJOYED ALL BUT MAYBE ONE OR TWO OF THEM. *THIS BOY'S LIFE* IS ONE OF MY FAVORITES. I KNOW WE LIVE QUITE FAR APART, BUT I WOULD LOVE TO KNOW MORE ABOUT YOU. AND OK, IF YOU'D LIKE TO SHARE ANY JUICY DETAILS ABOUT YOUR CARMEN ELECTRA INTERVIEW, I WOULDN'T THINK LESS OF YOU.   —BEN

I RESPONDED RIGHT AWAY. SOON, WE WERE EXCHANGING DAILY MISSIVES.

WOW, YOU'RE TURNING ME ON WITH ALL THIS BOOK TALK. I AM A GIGANTIC PHILIP ROTH FAN. I'VE PROBABLY READ MORE OF HIM THAN ANY OTHER AUTHOR.

EVERY AFTERNOON I RAN HOME TO SEE IF HE'D WRITTEN.

I'M JUST HAPPY THAT BASEBALL SEASON IS GOING TO START SOON. I LOVE FOLLOWING THE BOX SCORES.

HE TOLD ME ABOUT HIS SISTER, WHO'D BEEN KILLED IN A CAR CRASH.

WOW ABOUT YOUR SISTER. ARE YOU FINDING IT DIFFICULT TO MAKE THE FILM ABOUT HER?

THE WHOLE STORY ABOUT YOUR FATHER IS JUST FASCINATING. YOU COULD SELL THE MOVIE RIGHTS TOMORROW IF YOU WANTED.

WE WERE BOTH ATTEMPTING TO MAKE ART OUT OF THE TRAGEDIES OF OUR FAMILY LIVES.

MY FATHER KNEW VERY WELL THAT I WAS WRITING THE STORY ABOUT HIM, BUT I THINK HE WAS IN SOME KIND OF DENIAL. I THINK HE FELT THAT BY TELLING HIS STORY TO A MAGAZINE IT WOULD BECOME REAL; IT WOULD BE LEGITIMIZED. AND I WAS IN MY OWN KIND OF DENIAL, BECAUSE I DIDN'T WANT TO DEBUNK THE MYTH AND POSSIBLY DESTROY OUR RELATIONSHIP.

MY HOURS AT WORK GREW LONGER. NIGHT AFTER NIGHT, I STAYED AT THE OFFICE, SOMETIMES UNTIL MIDNIGHT OR LATER, WORKING ON MY CELEBRITY INTERVIEWS.

YOU'RE STILL HERE?

WHAT WAS THERE TO RUSH HOME TO? I'D MOVED TO MY OWN APARTMENT IN BROOKLYN, BUT I HAD NO HUSBAND OR KIDS, NO PETS, NOT EVEN A PLANT.

I **DID** HAVE BEN, BUT BEN WAS PORTABLE.

I DON'T OFTEN GET LONELY. I THINK THE MOST LONELY I'VE EVER FELT WAS WHEN I WAS IN A RELATIONSHIP THAT WASN'T WORKING.

EVENTUALLY, I WAS SENT OUT TO L.A. AGAIN.

UNLESS HE'S QUASIMODO, I'M SLEEPING WITH HIM.

GENEVIEVE FIELD

BEN AND I SPOKE ON THE PHONE FOR THE FIRST TIME THE NIGHT BEFORE I FLEW TO L.A. I SWALLOWED MY NERVOUSNESS AND PRETENDED I WAS THE MOST CONFIDENT PERSON IN THE WORLD. HE WAS JUST AS ENGAGING ON THE PHONE AS HE WAS IN HIS E-MAILS.

SO I PLANNED ACCORDINGLY.

SEXY THONGS

CONDOMS

CONTROLLED SUBSTANCE
PHARMACY
URIE A. SANDEL
AMBIEN 10mg
TAKE AS NEEDED
SMITH ST

102

THE NIGHT I ARRIVED, WE MET AT THE BAR IN THE FOUR SEASONS HOTEL. WHEN WE FINALLY SAW EACH OTHER, I HAD TO READJUST MY MENTAL IMAGE OF HIM. HE WAS TALL AND HANDSOME BUT **SO** NOT MY TYPE. I LIKED SCRUFFY ARTIST-TYPE GUYS. HE WAS CLEAN-CUT, WITH A SQUARE JAW AND A CLEFT CHIN — AN EVEN MANLIER GEORGE CLOONEY.

HE WAS ALMOST **TOO** HANDSOME, IN A WAY THAT HAD ME WONDERING IF HE'D EVER BEEN SCREAMED AT IN THE BASEMENT BY HIS FATHER, HAD HIS ARM GRABBED AND SQUEEZED LIKE SOMEONE WAS TAKING HIS BLOOD PRESSURE, OR BEEN THE TARGET OF A SPEEDING BOTTLE OF TAB.

SO, DO YOU LIKE L.A.?

I DO. IT CAN BE A STRANGE PLACE, THOUGH.

WELL, I'M PRETTY ATTACHED TO NEW YORK. THERE'S SOMETHING ABOUT THE CITY THAT FEELS GRITTY BUT REAL, LIKE MY FAVORITE LINE FROM THAT LEONARD COHEN SONG, "CHELSEA HOTEL." "WE ARE UGLY, BUT WE HAVE THE MUSIC."

I GET IT. I LOVE NEW YORK. WHENEVER I VISIT, THERE IS A PART OF ME THAT FEELS REALLY AT HOME.

LATER, I INVITED HIM UP TO MY ROOM. WE LAY ON THE BED, FACING EACH OTHER, TALKING FOR HOURS. HE STILL DIDN'T MAKE A MOVE.

104

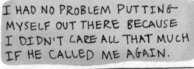

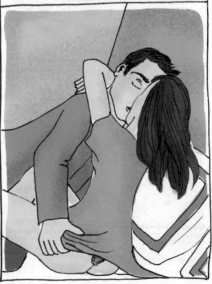

I HAD NO PROBLEM PUTTING MYSELF OUT THERE BECAUSE I DIDN'T CARE ALL THAT MUCH IF HE CALLED ME AGAIN.

FROM THE MINUTE I MET HIM, I HAD A SUBTLE SENSE THAT *I* HAD THE UPPER HAND. REAL OR IMAGINED, IT DIDN'T MATTER: THAT FEELING OF CONTROL ALLOWED ME TO LET DOWN MY GUARD.

YOU'VE GOT A GREAT ASS.

THANK YOU.

LOVE, LUST, INFATUATION — THEY HAD ALWAYS BEEN TOO SCARY FOR ME. WHENEVER THOSE FEELINGS CROPPED UP, I LOST MYSELF INSTANTLY.

DID I... DID I WAKE YOU?

HUH?

TAP TAP

Maise

THE ANTIDOTE, I'D FOUND, WAS TO ENSURE I NEVER FELT VULNERABLE. I DID THAT BY DATING MEN WHO LIKED ME MORE THAN I LIKED THEM.

I HAVE TO GO BUT I DON'T WANT TO.

I'LL KEEP YOUR SIDE OF THE BED WARM.

WHEN I RETURNED TO NEW YORK, I SENT BEN A LIGHT, JOKEY E-MAIL.

IF I WAS DRIVING A RENTAL CAR FROM THE FOUR SEASONS TO THE L'ERMITAGE HOTEL AND THE WIND VELOCITY WAS 65 MPH, HOW LONG WOULD IT TAKE ME TO GET THERE IF I DIDN'T KNOW HOW TO TURN ON THE RENTAL CAR'S HEADLIGHTS, LET ALONE DRIVE FROM POINT A TO POINT B?

BUT SOMEHOW, IT WASN'T THE SAME. BEN WANTED MORE.

I'M BACK FROM SAN DIEGO ON SUNDAY. MAYBE I'LL GIVE YOU A CALL. I FEEL LIKE OUR RELATIONSHIP CAN HANDLE THE OCCASIONAL PHONE CALL NOW, RIGHT?

MEANWHILE, AT WORK, I SCORED MY NEXT BIG ASSIGNMENT. IT WAS OUR OCTOBER COVER STORY, AN IN-PERSON INTERVIEW WITH ASHLEY JUDD. THE INTERVIEW WAS SCHEDULED FOR TWO DAYS FROM THEN.

RESEARCH

BEN HAD DECIDED TO VISIT ME IN NEW YORK, AND IT WAS TOO LATE TO CHANGE HIS TICKET. THE DAY HE ARRIVED, I GOT ON A PLANE. WE DIDN'T EVEN GET TO SAY HELLO TO ONE ANOTHER.

THE INTERVIEW TOOK PLACE IN DETROIT, WHERE JUDD'S HUSBAND, A RACECAR DRIVER, WAS PARTICIPATING IN A QUALIFYING RACE.

MICHIGAN INTERNATIONAL SPEEDWAY

THAT WAY.

I OPENED THE DOOR TO HER TRAILER TO FIND HER SITTING AT A TINY LITTLE TABLE. SHE WAS **BEAUTIFUL** AND TRULY LOOKED LIKE A MOVIE STAR: SHE WORE A TANGLE OF DIAMOND NECKLACES, AND HER HAIR WAS ARTFULLY TOUSLED.

NERVOUS WRECK

BUTTERMILK, *NO*!

I TRIED TO ACT NATURAL WHILE SHE FINISHED UP WORK ON HER COMPUTER.

NOWHERE TO PUT LEFT HAND.

WHEN THE INTERVIEW BEGAN, I WAS IMMEDIATELY IN OVER MY HEAD. I'D BEEN SENT THERE TO GET HER TO ANSWER STYLE QUESTIONS. ALL SHE WANTED TO TALK ABOUT WAS HER RECENT TRIP TO THAILAND FOR CHARITY.

HERE'S A PICTURE OF MILA, A BROTHEL SEX SLAVE I WAS ABLE TO SAVE. HER LIFE WAS A DISASTER.

WOW, UM... WHAT'S YOUR BIGGEST *FASHION* DISASTER?

AS I SCANNED MY QUESTIONS, I FELT HER SLIPPING AWAY.

THEN I DUG UP AN OLD TECHNIQUE.

I'M ALSO WORKING ON A BOOK ABOUT MY DAD.

OH? WHAT ABOUT?

ONCE AGAIN, MY DAD'S STORIES, WHICH WERE BECOMING *MY* STORY, MANAGED TO TURN A CONVERSATION AROUND.

WE FINISHED THE INTERVIEW. THAT SAME DAY, I FLEW BACK TO NEW YORK TO SEE BEN.

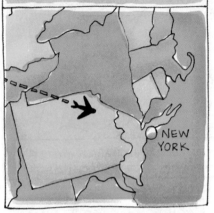

I DIDN'T ARRIVE UNTIL MIDNIGHT BUT HAD THE CAR SERVICE DROP ME OFF AT A NICE RESTAURANT IN SOHO, SO I COULD TELL BEN EVERY DETAIL OF MY INTERVIEW.

IT WAS SO GOOD TO SEE HIM! HE OPENED HIS ARMS AND FOLDED ME INTO A HUGE BEAR HUG.

OH MY GOD. THAT IS SO COOL. TELL ME MORE.

THEN I WAS LIKE, "WHAT'S YOUR BIGGEST FASHION DISASTER?"

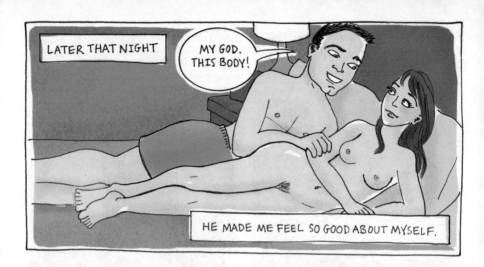

LATER THAT NIGHT

MY GOD. THIS BODY!

HE MADE ME FEEL SO GOOD ABOUT MYSELF.

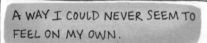

A WAY I COULD NEVER SEEM TO FEEL ON MY OWN.

FLAT CHEST

BIG EARS

INGROWN HAIR

KNOBBY KNEES

BEN FELL ASLEEP WITHIN MINUTES. I NEEDED HELP.

THE NEXT MORNING

I'D NEVER FELT SO CONFIDENT. SO PRETTY. SO SEXY. STILL, IN THE LIGHT OF DAY, WITHOUT WINE OR AMBIEN IN MY SYSTEM, THERE SEEMED TO BE SOMETHING MISSING.

I DIDN'T KNOW WHAT IT WAS. BUT I DIDN'T HAVE TO THINK ABOUT IT FOR LONG: HE LEFT THE NEXT DAY.

BY EVENING, I HAD FORGOTTEN MY MISGIVINGS. I FANTASIZED ABOUT THE IDYLLIC TIME WE'D HAD TOGETHER.

I FELL ASLEEP AT 2:30 A.M., WITH THE PHONE IN MY HAND, AFTER A MARATHON TALK WITH BEN.

AND TWO AMBIEN.

WHEN I WENT TO WORK ON MONDAY, I GOT AN E-MAIL FROM ASHLEY JUDD.

HOLY SHIT!

SHE SAID SHE'D ENJOYED MEETING ME AND THOUGHT I WAS BRAVE FOR WRITING ABOUT MY DAD. I WAS FLOATING ON AIR! **ASHLEY JUDD** HAD SENT **ME** A PERSONAL E-MAIL, UNRELATED TO WORK!

I E-MAILED BACK RIGHT AWAY, AND SHE E-MAILED ME BACK WITH **BOOK** RECOMMENDATIONS!

HA!

WHO'S THAT FROM?

OH, IT'S JUST ASHLEY JUDD. SHE E-MAILS ME SOMETIMES.

NO WAY!

WAY.

I LET IT SLIP TO MY EDITOR THAT ASHLEY JUDD AND I WERE SENDING E-MAILS BACK AND FORTH. SHE LET IT SLIP TO THE BOSS. SOON, I WAS DOING **ALL** THE CELEBRITY INTERVIEWS FOR THE MAGAZINE, FLYING ACROSS THE COUNTRY ON A MONTHLY BASIS, STAYING IN HOTELS WITH OVAL-SHAPED POOLS AND FLUFFY BATHROBES AND FIVE-THOUSAND-THREAD-COUNT SHEETS.

THE NIGHTLY PHONE CALLS WITH BEN TURNED INTO A FULL-FLEDGED LONG-DISTANCE RELATIONSHIP. I SAW HIM EVERY TIME I WAS IN L.A.

AND EVERY TIME I STARTED TO FEEL A PRICK OF DOUBT ABOUT HIM, IT WAS TIME TO LEAVE.

DOUBT

WITHIN MONTHS, I BECAME A REGULAR AT THE CHATEAU MARMONT HOTEL. SOMETIMES, THE GUYS AT THE FRONT DESK KNEW MY NAME AND UPGRADED ME TO A HUGE ONE-BEDROOM SUITE.

OTHER TIMES, THEY HAD NO IDEA WHO I WAS AND ACTED REALLY SNOBBY.

THE ONE THING THAT MADE IT OK TO GO TO L.A. SO OFTEN WAS VISITING BEN. I WOULD HAVE BEEN SO LONELY AMONG THOSE FLASHY, FAKE PEOPLE WITHOUT HIM.

THE ONLY THING WAS I WAS KIND OF LONELY **WITH** HIM TOO. I COULDN'T PUT MY FINGER ON THE REASON WHY.

HE WAS THE MOST THOUGHTFUL GUY I'D EVER MET.

HE WAS GREAT IN BED.

HE'D READ MORE THAN ANYONE I'D EVER MET — PERHAPS EVEN MY FATHER.

I WAS 100 PERCENT **MYSELF** WITH HIM.

YET I TREATED THE RELATIONSHIP AS A CASUAL THING.

OH, NO, IT'S NOT SERIOUS.

MY FRIENDS COULDN'T UNDERSTAND MY HESITATION. WHEN I TRIED TO EXPLAIN MY DOUBTS, THEY SOUNDED RIDICULOUS.

"HE'S TOO CLEAN—CUT."

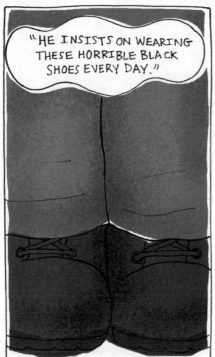

"HE INSISTS ON WEARING THESE HORRIBLE BLACK SHOES EVERY DAY."

"HIS CAR IS SO **BIG**."

TO ME, THOSE CHOICES SIGNALED A LACK OF POETRY IN HIS SOUL, A MARRIAGE TO THE CONCRETE.

TWO ON, TWO OUT. CLEMENS DEALS TO ORTIZ.

IT WAS A QUALITY THAT BOTH ATTRACTED AND REPULSED ME. IT WAS WHAT I IMAGINED I'D HAVE TO ACCEPT IF I EVER WANTED TO HAVE A HEALTHY RELATIONSHIP.

BUT I COULDN'T.

WHERE ARE YOU GOING?

I HADN'T YET KICKED MY ATTRACTION TO LARGER-THAN-LIFE NARCISSISTS, AND BEN WAS SO... WELL... *NORMAL*.

ONE ON, TWO OUT, ONE RUN IN. VARITEK STEPS TO THE PLATE.

117

HE WAS MY BROCCOLI.

GOOD FOR ME!

WAS IT POSSIBLE I WASN'T IN LOVE WITH BEN BECAUSE HE WASN'T *ENOUGH* LIKE MY DAD? CHARMING... WILDLY PASSIONATE... MERCURIAL...

HE SAID, "YOU INSULTED THE UNIFORM OF THE REPUBLIC OF ARGENTINA!" I WAS IMMEDIATELY ARRESTED.

ALL I KNEW WAS THAT WHENEVER WE WERE APART, I MISSED BEN LIKE CRAZY.

BUT EVERY TIME WE SPENT MORE THAN A FEW DAYS TOGETHER, I FELT SUFFOCATED AND FOUND MYSELF PICKING ON HIM.

YOU'RE GOING TO WEAR **THAT** T-SHIRT?

AFTERWARD, I FELT TERRIBLE.

NO, YOU SHOULD WEAR IT. HONESTLY, IT LOOKS GREAT.

AND CONVINCED MYSELF OUR ISSUES WERE MY FAULT.

WHAT DO YOU MEAN, YOU DON'T WANT KIDS?

I DON'T HAVE THAT URGE: I LIKE MY LIFE THE WAY IT IS.

LUCKILY, THERE WERE SO MANY DISTRACTIONS IN L.A., I DIDN'T HAVE TO DEAL WITH MY FEELINGS FOR TOO LONG.

OOH, LOOK— KIRSTEN DUNST!

KITSON

OVER THE NEXT FEW MONTHS, MY JOB GOT EVEN MORE DEMANDING.

IN MY SPARE TIME, I WAS STILL INVESTIGATING MY FATHER'S PAST.

MOST SATURDAYS, AT THE NEW YORK PUBLIC LIBRARY.

NEW LAPTOP ▷

I FOUND MYSELF RELYING ON MY FATHER'S STORIES MORE AND MORE TO CONNECT WITH FAMOUS PEOPLE.

I'M ACTUALLY WORKING ON A BOOK ABOUT MY DAD. HE'S STILL MARRIED TO MY MOM, BUT I RECENTLY FOUND OUT HE'S A CON ARTIST.

LAURA DERN

TAPE RECORDER

FORGET ABOUT *MY* STORY — TELL ME *YOURS!*

OVER TIME, I SAT DOWN WITH A VIRTUAL

1. MEG RYAN 2. SUSAN SARANDON 3. JENNIFER LOPEZ 4. UMA THURMAN
5. KELLY RIPA 6. ALANIS MORISSETTE 7. LARA FLYNN BOYLE 8. KATE WINSLET
9. NICOLE RICHIE 10. HALLE BERRY 11. NAOMI WATTS 12. JENNIFER GARNER
13. NATALIE PORTMAN 14. TERRI HATCHER 15. JESSICA ALBA 16. KATIE HOLMES
17. TYRA BANKS 18. JENNIFER CONNELLY 19. JESSICA SIMPSON
20. SALMA HAYEK 21. EVA MENDES 22. CHRISTINA AGUILERA

THOUGH I AFFECTED INDIFFERENCE DURING INTERVIEWS, I WAS **DAZZLED** IN THE PRESENCE OF CELEBRITY. THERE WAS SOME— THING ABOUT BEING CHOSEN TO SIT DOWN WITH A PERSON WHO MILLIONS OF PEOPLE WANTED TO TALK TO, TO BE SEEN AT **HER** TABLE — AN INVITED GUEST — THAT WAS THRILLING FOR ME.

KATHERINE HEIGL

THE FEELING WAS FAMILIAR.

THE BIG GUNS

IT HAD BEEN A YEAR SINCE THE STORY ON MY FATHER HAD COME OUT, TWO YEARS SINCE WE'D SPOKEN. AT TIMES, I FORGOT THAT I **HAD** A REAL FATHER: HE EXISTED IN THE STORIES I TOLD ALONE.

YOU'RE **KIDDING!**

CATHERINE ZETA-JONES

FOR THE MOST PART, THAT DIDN'T BOTHER ME, EXCEPT DURING CERTAIN HOLIDAYS.

WHAT'S ALL THAT NOISE IN THE BACKGROUND?

WE'RE OUT TO DINNER FOR FATHER'S DAY. ARE YOU UPSET?

WHENEVER I MET MY MOTHER FOR LUNCH, I TOLD HER NOTHING ABOUT WHAT I WAS DOING AND ASKED NOTHING OF HER IN RETURN. SHE THOUGHT THE STORY WAS SAFELY PUT TO BED.

SO WHO ARE YOU INTERVIEWING NEXT?

DAD'S — I MEAN, NAOMI CAMPBELL.

IT WASN'T, OF COURSE. EVERY TIME I LIFTED THE LID ON MY FATHER'S LIFE, THOUSANDS OF CLUES CAME TUMBLING OUT, ONLY TO CREATE MORE QUESTIONS. BUT NOTHING ALLOWED ME TO YANK BACK THE WIZARD OF OZ—LIKE CURTAIN TO REVEAL HIS TRUE SELF.

I WANTED TO KNOW EVERYTHING. THIS ELUSIVE INFORMATION, I WAS SURE, HELD THE KEY TO MY FUTURE HAPPINESS. ALL THOSE MISSING PIECES, THE FEELING I DIDN'T BELONG, THE SUSPICION THAT I WAS DIFFERENT.... IT WOULD ALL MAKE SENSE.

BUT I NEEDED HELP.

A.R.M. ASSOCIATES, INC.

PRIVATE INVESTIGATIONS

Albert R. McEvoy
President
Former Police Commissioner
Yonkers, New York
Licensed/Bonded/Insured
New York State

Phone: 914-964-5734
Fax: 914-517-5900
piarmassoc@aol.com
Post Office Box 147
Yonkers, NY 10703

I THOUGHT ABOUT THE FILE THAT PI HAD TO HAVE ON MY FATHER, TWELVE INCHES THICK. I *HAD* TO HAVE THAT FILE.

HELLO?

HOW ARE YA? AL MCEVOY HERE.

AL! HELLO!

LISTEN, I'M SORRY I DIDN'T GET BACK TO YOU SOONER. I WAS IN FLORIDA PLAYING GOLF AND HADN'T CHECKED MY NEW YORK MESSAGES IN A WHILE.

SO DO YOU REMEMBER MY DAD?

OF COURSE, I DO. SEEMED LIKE AN INTERESTING GUY.

WE MADE A PLAN TO MEET THE FOLLOWING THURSDAY NIGHT.

LET'S MEET AT THE STAMFORD TRAIN STATION. WE CAN MEET ON THE PLATFORM.

WHAT WILL YOU LOOK LIKE?

YOU'LL KNOW ME. I LOOK LIKE A RETIRED COP.

THE DAY OF OUR MEETING, I RACED OUT OF WORK TO CATCH THE 5:53 P.M. TRAIN TO STAMFORD, FEELING LIKE I WAS STARRING IN A MOVIE ABOUT MY OWN LIFE.

IN THE RESTAURANT...

Giulia, Dad's secretary
Timmy B., ham radio
friend (has spina
bifida, in wheelchair)
Gustavo Torres, old friend
of my father's (stands
at least 6'7")
Marcus Kipplinger,
Dad's first cousin
Mai Feng, my dad's
"email infatuation"
feng@hotmail...

I HANDED HIM A LIST OF PEOPLE I
WANTED TO FIND.

I DID A PRELIMINARY SEARCH:
I'VE ALREADY FOUND THREE
OR FOUR LAWSUITS AGAINST
YOUR FATHER — AND ONE
AGAINST YOUR MOTHER — AS
WELL AS A BANK PROBLEM AND
AN APPLICATION FOR A LOAN.

WAIT A MINUTE —
THERE'S A LAWSUIT
FILED AGAINST
MY *MOTHER*?

YEAH, SOMETHING
TO DO WITH A
DINERS CLUB CARD
SHE DIDN'T PAY.

MY MOTHER WAS AN ABSOLUTE
SQUARE — SHE'D NEVER HAD SO
MUCH AS A PARKING TICKET.

129

OVER THE NEXT FEW WEEKS, AL TIED UP ALL THE LOOSE ENDS.

FEBRUARY 20, 2:35 P.M.: NO LUCK WITH MAI FENG — SORRY. ALL THE TRAILS WENT DEAD.

FEBRUARY 29, 5:19 P.M.: FOUND JIMMY B.!

MARCH 5, 1:23 P.M.: HERE'S GIULIA'S ADDRESS. GOOD LUCK.

HE'D SUGGESTED I SEND LETTERS TO THE PEOPLE HE WAS ABLE TO TRACK DOWN. I MAILED OFF THE LETTERS.

THE THREE LAWSUITS HE FOUND AGAINST MY PARENTS WERE FROM THE DINERS CLUB, THE GUY WHO'D BOUGHT OUR HOUSE AT AUCTION, AND A WALTER MATHESON OF CHAPPAQUA, NEW YORK.

ANY IDEA WHO THIS MATHESON GUY IS?

HE WAS MY MOM'S BEST FRIEND'S HUSBAND. I HADN'T SEEN HIM IN YEARS.

HI, GIRLS.

SEARCHING FOR THE TRUTH ABOUT MY FATHER WAS LIKE DIGGING AT THE BEACH. THE MORE I DUG, THE MORE THE HOLE KEPT FILLING UP WITH WATER.

WALTER, HOW ARE YA?

130

THE TOWEL

IN JUNE, BEN CAME TO VISIT ME IN NEW YORK. THE
WEEKEND WAS GREAT, UNTIL . . .

I FELT LIKE I WAS BEING CHOKED BY THAT TOWEL — I
COULDN'T BREATHE.

DO YOU GET AN AIRPORT CONNECTION? I CAN'T SEE THE GODDAM BASEBALL SCORES.

WHERE DO YOU WANT TO GO TO DINNER TONIGHT?

BLUE RIBBON, MAYBE?

LATER THAT NIGHT AFTER SEVERAL GLASSES OF WINE, I FELT FLUSHED AND HAPPY.

BEFORE I CRAWLED INTO BED WITH HIM, I SECRETLY TOOK AMBIEN.

I DON'T KNOW WHY I HID IT FROM HIM — I'D TAKEN AMBIEN WITH HIS KNOWLEDGE BEFORE, DURING OUR ENDLESS PHONE CONVERSATIONS.

I DID IT AS A WAY TO FORCE MYSELF OFF OF THE PHONE WHEN I HAD TO WORK THE NEXT DAY. BUT IT DIDN'T ALWAYS WORK OUT THAT WAY. MOST OF THOSE AMBIEN-FUELED CONVERSATIONS HAD LED TO UNCONSCIOUS PHONE SEX.

I'M NAKED AND TOUCHING MYSELF...

WHICH I WAS REALLY GOOD AT, I HEAR.

I DID **WHAT** LAST NIGHT? NO, NO, I REMEMBER.

STILL, I SUPPOSE I KNEW HE WOULDN'T BE TOO KEEN ON THE IDEA OF ACTUAL SEX WITH A COMATOSE WOMAN.

JUST BEFORE I SCREWED THE CAP BACK ON, I LOOKED IN THE BOTTLE: I WAS DOWN TO MY LAST ONE! HOW HAD I RUN OUT SO QUICKLY?

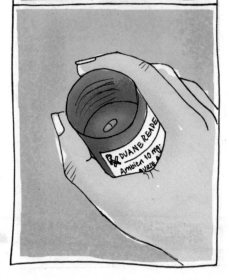

133

THEN THE AMBIEN KICKED IN. I FELT DROWSILY HOT FOR HIM, WARM ALL OVER, AND, OF COURSE, EXPERIMENTAL.

WANNA GET ON THE FLOOR AND **SPANK** ME?

WHOA. OK.

DID YOU TAKE AMBIEN? YOU'RE ACTING WEIRD.

NO.

RIDE 'EM, COWBOY!

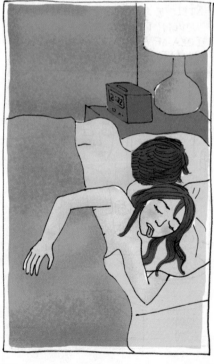

IN THE MORNING, I FELT ANXIOUS AGAIN.

YOU WERE GREAT LAST NIGHT.

THANKS . . . ?

I COULDN'T REMEMBER A *THING* THAT WE'D DONE — AFTER THE SPANKING, ANYWAY.

WE SPENT THE DAY LOUNGING AROUND MY APARTMENT. HE DIDN'T SAY A WORD ABOUT THE STATE I'D BEEN IN HOURS EARLIER.

135

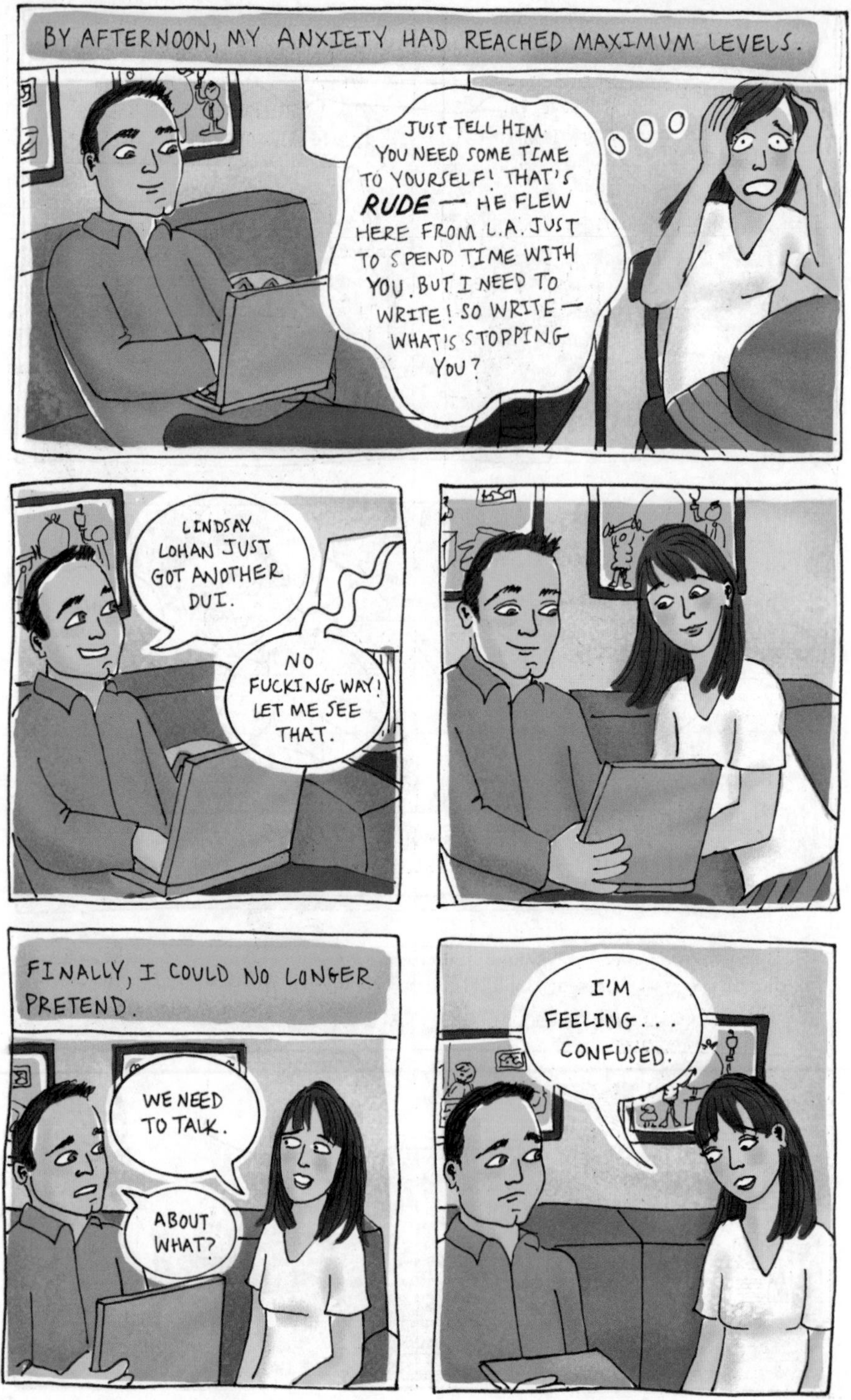
BY AFTERNOON, MY ANXIETY HAD REACHED MAXIMUM LEVELS.
JUST TELL HIM YOU NEED SOME TIME TO YOURSELF! THAT'S **RUDE** — HE FLEW HERE FROM L.A. JUST TO SPEND TIME WITH YOU. BUT I NEED TO WRITE! SO WRITE — WHAT'S STOPPING YOU?
LINDSAY LOHAN JUST GOT ANOTHER DUI.
NO FUCKING WAY! LET ME SEE THAT.
FINALLY, I COULD NO LONGER PRETEND.
WE NEED TO TALK.
ABOUT WHAT?
I'M FEELING... CONFUSED.

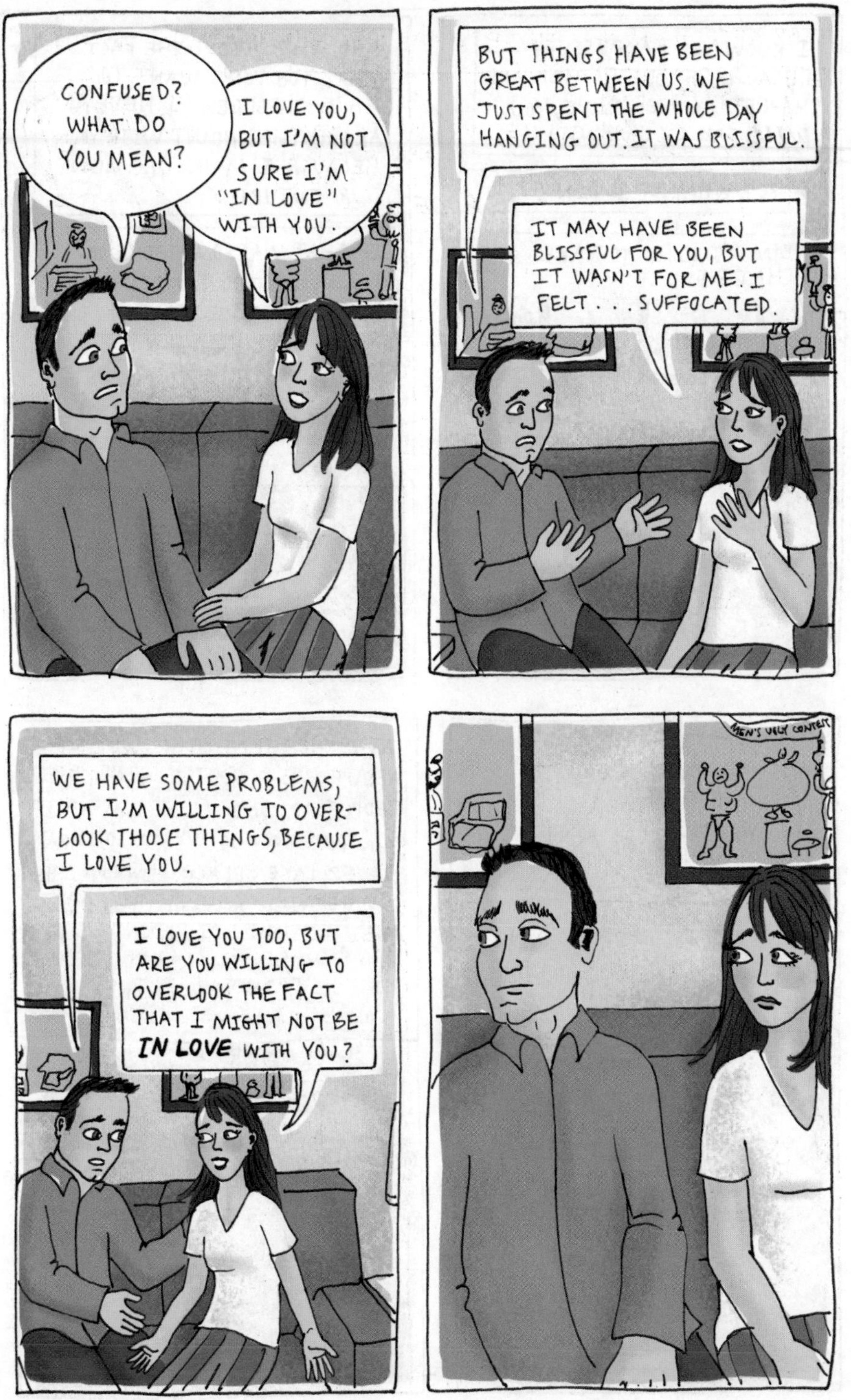
CONFUSED? WHAT DO YOU MEAN?
I LOVE YOU, BUT I'M NOT SURE I'M "IN LOVE" WITH YOU.
BUT THINGS HAVE BEEN GREAT BETWEEN US. WE JUST SPENT THE WHOLE DAY HANGING OUT. IT WAS BLISSFUL.
IT MAY HAVE BEEN BLISSFUL FOR YOU, BUT IT WASN'T FOR ME. I FELT . . . SUFFOCATED.
WE HAVE SOME PROBLEMS, BUT I'M WILLING TO OVER-LOOK THOSE THINGS, BECAUSE I LOVE YOU.
I LOVE YOU TOO, BUT ARE YOU WILLING TO OVERLOOK THE FACT THAT I MIGHT NOT BE **IN LOVE** WITH YOU?
MEN'S UGLY CONTEST

I KNOW YOU HAVE ISSUES BECAUSE OF YOUR FATHER, AND HOPEFULLY, OVER TIME, YOU **WILL** FALL IN LOVE WITH ME.

BUT WHAT IF I DON'T?

I'M WILLING TO TAKE THAT RISK.

AND WHAT ABOUT THE FACT THAT YOU DON'T WANT TO HAVE CHILDREN? I NEVER ARGUE THAT POINT WITH YOU BECAUSE I'M UNSURE ABOUT OUR FUTURE.

IF THAT WAS SOMETHING YOU REALLY WANTED, I WOULDN'T ASK YOU TO GIVE THAT UP.

SO YOU'D HAVE KIDS YOU DIDN'T WANT?

FOR YOU, I WOULD.

AT DINNER THAT NIGHT, WE CHATTED ABOUT THE FOOD, THE WINE, THE PEOPLE AROUND US. IT WAS AS IF OUR PREVIOUS CONVERSATION HAD NEVER TAKEN PLACE. HOW COULD HE SAY HE WAS OK WITH THE FACT THAT I MIGHT NOT BE IN LOVE WITH HIM? OR BE WILLING TO BRING KIDS HE DIDN'T WANT INTO THE WORLD?

138

THAT NIGHT I SLEPT FITFULLY — I DIDN'T WANT TO TAKE MY LAST AMBIEN.

AS SOON AS HE LEFT FOR THE AIRPORT THE NEXT MORNING, THE TRAPPED SENSATION I'D BEEN FEELING ALL WEEKEND SUBSIDED.

I HAD TWO DIFFERENT DOCTORS CALL IN PRESCRIPTIONS FOR AMBIEN AND ASKED MY MOTHER, THE CONSUMMATE NONADDICT, TO SEND A FEW EXTRAS FROM HER BARELY USED STASH TO TIDE ME OVER.

HOW MANY DO YOU NEED?

UM, TEN OR SO? I'M NOT SURE WHEN I'LL BE ABLE TO GET TO THE PHARMACY.

IN NOVEMBER, BEN VISITED ME IN NEW YORK AGAIN. WE PLANNED TO SPEND A FEW DAYS TOGETHER, THEN TRAVEL TO HIS PARENTS' HOUSE IN BOSTON FOR THANKSGIVING. IT DIDN'T TAKE LONG FOR ME TO FEEL THE WALLS CLOSING IN.

IN CENTRAL PARK

AT DINNER

WHAT'S WRONG?

NOTHING.

THE NIGHT BEFORE WE LEFT FOR HIS PARENTS', THE FEELING INTENSIFIED. I WAS COOKING MY SPECIALTY, CHICKEN POT PIE.

I CAN'T DO THIS!

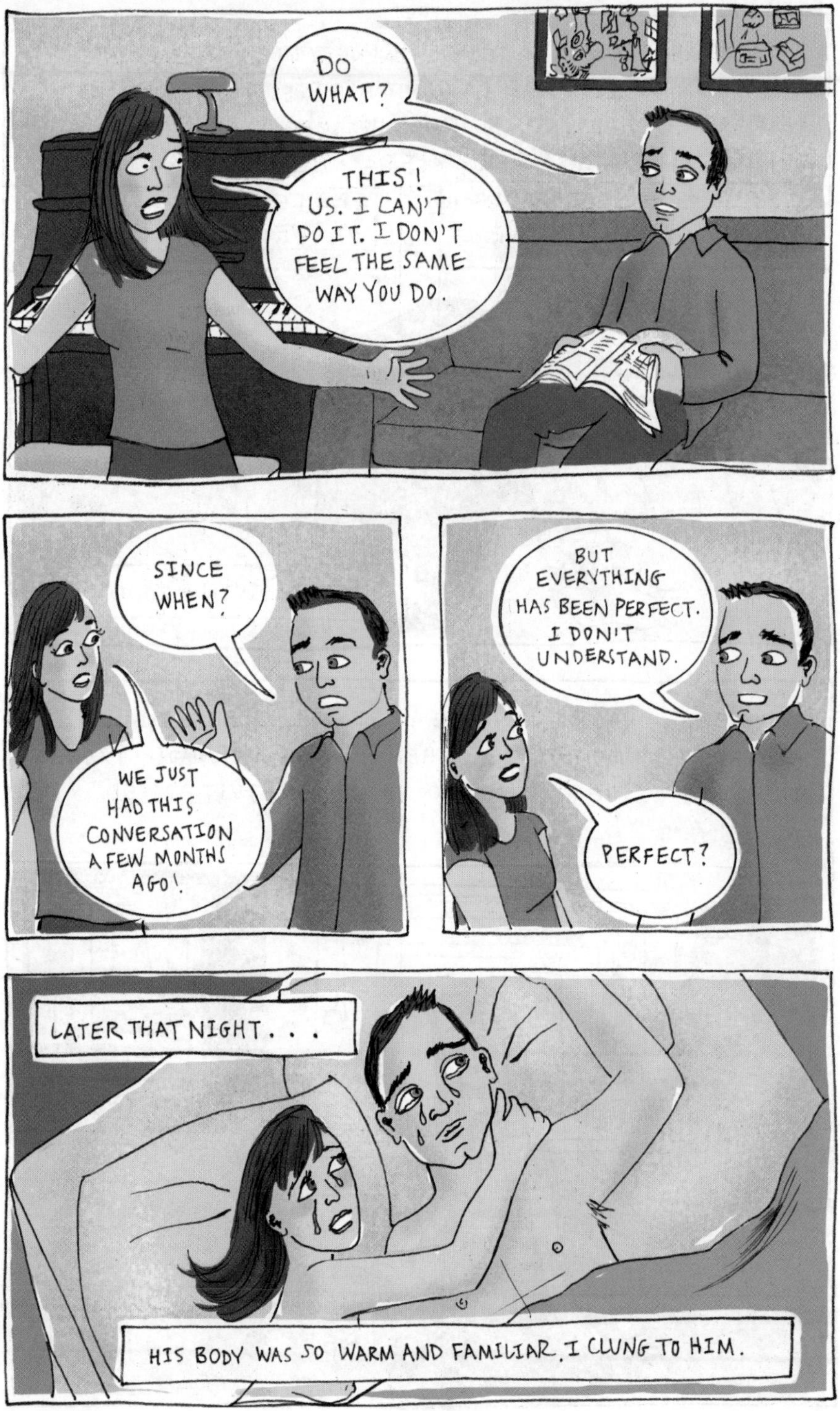
DO WHAT?
THIS! US. I CAN'T DO IT. I DON'T FEEL THE SAME WAY YOU DO.
SINCE WHEN?
WE JUST HAD THIS CONVERSATION A FEW MONTHS AGO!
BUT EVERYTHING HAS BEEN PERFECT. I DON'T UNDERSTAND.
PERFECT?
LATER THAT NIGHT . . .
HIS BODY WAS SO WARM AND FAMILIAR. I CLUNG TO HIM.

I THOUGHT I'D DONE THE RIGHT THING. I LOVED HIM, BUT I NEEDED TO BE **IN** LOVE. I WANTED TO FEEL MY STOMACH LURCH WHEN HE WAS AROUND; TO HAVE TROUBLE SLEEPING NOT BECAUSE I WAS MISERABLE BUT BECAUSE I WAS EXHILARATED; TO BE WILLING TO THROW MYSELF IN FRONT OF A TRUCK FOR HIM — OR **UNDER** ONE IF HE EVER LEFT ME.

THANKSGIVING 2005

AND YET, I WAS BACK WHERE I STARTED. THE MAN I WANTED TO KNOW — MY FATHER — WAS AS REMOTE FROM ME AS EVER. THE MAN CLOSEST TO ME, I'D JUST TOSSED OVERBOARD.

142

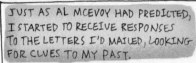

JUST AS AL MCEVOY HAD PREDICTED, I STARTED TO RECEIVE RESPONSES TO THE LETTERS I'D MAILED, LOOKING FOR CLUES TO MY PAST.

"YOUR LETTER CAME AS QUITE A SURPRISE."

WALTER MATHESON

I CALLED HIM.

ONE DAY, I GOT A PHONE CALL FROM YOUR DAD.

CAN YOU MEET ME BY THE DRESS BARN IN THE WHITE PLAINS MALL IN TWO HOURS?

WHAT'S THIS ALL ABOUT?

I'LL EXPLAIN LATER.

"GETTING A PHONE CALL OUT OF THE BLUE TO MEET AT A SECRET LOCATION. . . . I HAVE TO ADMIT, IT WAS KIND OF EXCITING. I MEAN, I'M A **DENTIST.**"

WHITE PLAINS MALL

A VERY GOOD BUSINESS DEAL HAS COME UP. HERE'S THE PROSPECTUS FOR THE COMPANY.

THE E.T.I. PROJECT

I'M GOING TO BE STRAIGHT WITH YOU. I NEED THIRTY THOUSAND DOLLARS TO BUY INTO THE COMPANY. I ALREADY HAVE SEVENTEEN THOUSAND DOLLARS OF THAT MONEY. WHAT I AM ASKING FROM YOU IS A LOAN FOR THE LAST THIRTEEN THOUSAND, IN EXCHANGE FOR ONE THOUSAND SHARES IN THE COMPANY. I CAN PAY YOU BACK IN TWO WEEKS.

WELL, I . . .

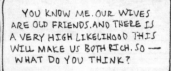
YOU KNOW ME. OUR WIVES ARE OLD FRIENDS. AND THERE IS A VERY HIGH LIKELIHOOD THIS WILL MAKE US BOTH RICH. SO — WHAT DO YOU THINK?

YOU **GAVE** IT TO HIM?

I HAPPENED TO HAVE THE MONEY IN MY SAVINGS ACCOUNT. I WROTE HIM A CHECK ON THE SPOT. DRIVING HOME, I THOUGHT, WHAT HAVE I DONE?

"TWO WEEKS WENT BY, THEN SIX MONTHS. FINALLY, BARBARA DISCOVERED THE DISCREPANCY IN OUR BANK BOOKS."

WHAT'S THIS?

SHE WAS REALLY ANGRY. BUT SHE'D BEEN FRIENDS WITH YOUR MOTHER SINCE HIGH SCHOOL, SO SHE DIDN'T WANT TO GET INVOLVED.

"WE STILL SAW YOUR PARENTS SOCIALLY. I NEVER BROUGHT UP THE MONEY BECAUSE YOUR FATHER ALWAYS BROUGHT IT UP FIRST."

THERE'S A BUSINESS DEAL COMING; YOUR MONEY IS ON THE WAY.

ALWAYS ANOTHER EXCUSE. FINALLY, I SAID, "ENOUGH," AND HANDED IT OVER TO AN ATTORNEY. IT TOOK TWO YEARS TO LITIGATE. IT BECAME VERY DIFFICULT FOR BARBARA TO STAY FRIENDS WITH YOUR MOM AFTER THAT.

LIKE MANY PEOPLE I'D SPOKEN TO, WALTER SEEMED TO FEEL ALMOST SORRY FOR MY FATHER.

YOUR DAD IS SUCH A SMART GUY. THERE WAS A TIME WHEN THINGS WERE GOING VERY WELL FOR HIM. HE HAD WHAT HE THOUGHT WAS THE MOST WONDERFUL JOB IN THE WORLD, AT RAMAPO COLLEGE. HE USED TO BRAG, "I WORK PART TIME; I HAVE A GREAT JOB WITH BENEFITS."

HE PAID CASH FOR THE HOUSE IN BRONXVILLE. AND I SAW SOME OF THE FURNITURE HE MADE — HE COULD HAVE MADE A GOOD LIVING AS A FURNITURE MAKER.

OVER THE NEXT MONTH, WALTER AND I SPOKE TWO MORE TIMES, AND HE ASKED ME TO SEND HIM A COPY OF MY ARTICLE ABOUT MY DAD. HE THANKED ME FOR SENDING IT, THEN OUR E-MAILS PETERED OUT. I WAS GLAD. I DIDN'T WANT TO STAY IN TOUCH: WHAT MY FATHER HAD DONE WAS TOO AWFUL.

I WAS BACK IN L.A. TO DO ANOTHER CELEBRITY INTERVIEW WHEN MY FATHER'S OLD FRIEND, GUSTAVO, CALLED.

SO, I KNOW YOU'RE STILL IN TOUCH WITH MY FATHER.

OH, HE CONSTANTLY SENDS ME POLITICAL ESSAYS.

THEN THIS MIGHT BE A LITTLE AWKWARD.

I HOPE YOU KNOW ME WELL ENOUGH TO LET YOUR GUARD DOWN AND TELL ME WHAT'S ON YOUR MIND.

AL MCEVOY HAD SUGGESTED I GIVE THE SMALLEST AMOUNT OF INFORMATION POSSIBLE TO GET SOMETHING BACK. BUT GUSTAVO WAS CRAFTY. HE ASKED JUST THE RIGHT QUESTIONS, AND I ENDED UP TELLING HIM ABOUT THE CREDIT CARDS, WALTER MATHESON, THE FORECLOSURE OF THE HOUSE.

COUPLE THINGS YOU NEED TO REALIZE. SOMEONE WHO HAS LIVED IN AS MANY DIFFERENT PLACES AS YOUR FATHER HAS... THERE'S ALWAYS BOUND TO BE PEOPLE TRYING TO GET AT HIM, TO SAY NEGATIVE THINGS.

I'VE NEVER HAD ANY MONEY BUSINESS WITH YOUR FATHER. I MET HIM MANY YEARS AGO INSTALLING A SECURITY SYSTEM IN A HOUSE IN ARDSLEY.

Chateau Marmont
8221 SUNSET BOULEVARD
HOLLYWOOD, CALIFORNIA 90046

On Dad's side!
installed security system
Ardsley

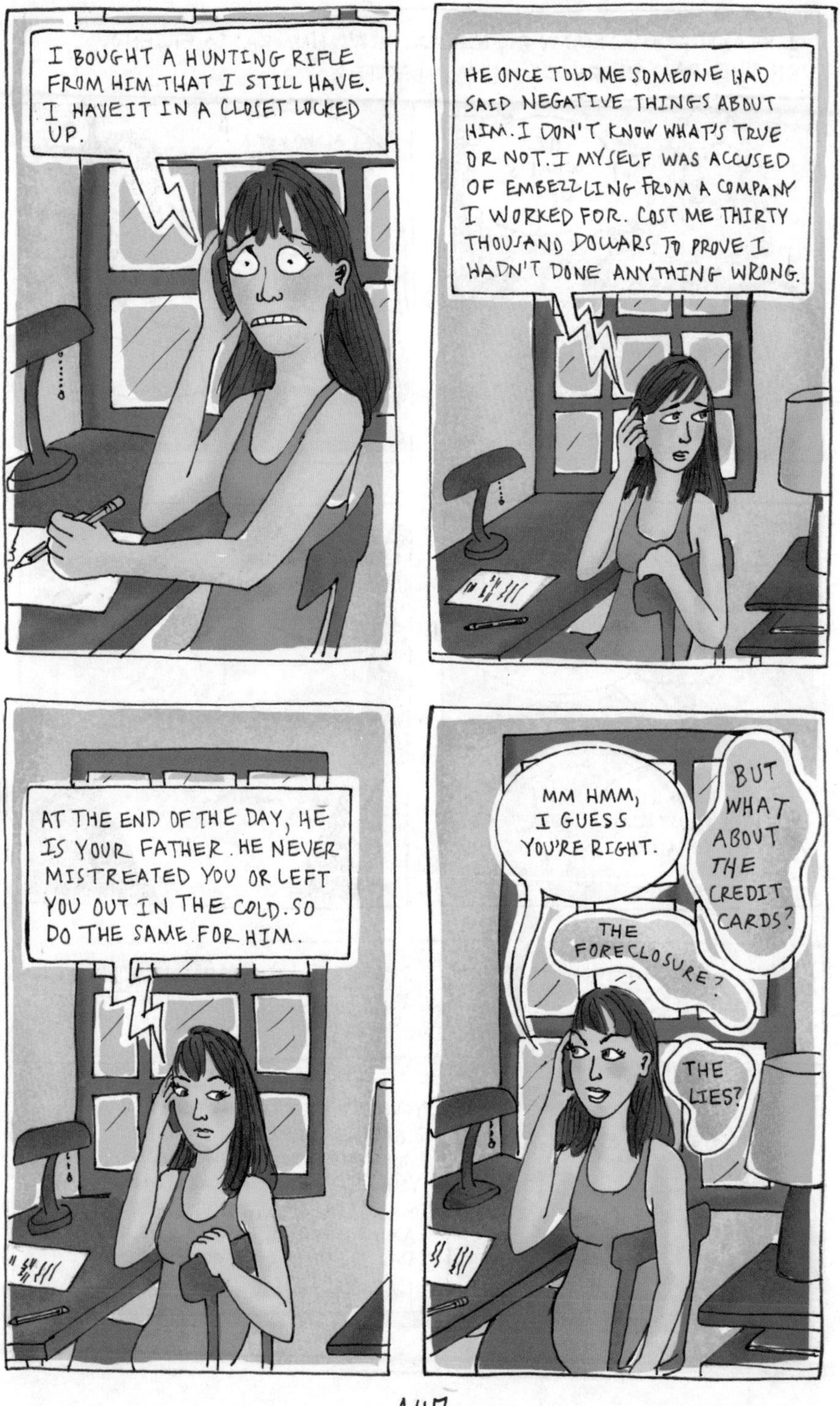
I BOUGHT A HUNTING RIFLE FROM HIM THAT I STILL HAVE. I HAVE IT IN A CLOSET LOCKED UP.
HE ONCE TOLD ME SOMEONE HAD SAID NEGATIVE THINGS ABOUT HIM. I DON'T KNOW WHAT'S TRUE OR NOT. I MYSELF WAS ACCUSED OF EMBEZZLING FROM A COMPANY I WORKED FOR. COST ME THIRTY THOUSAND DOLLARS TO PROVE I HADN'T DONE ANYTHING WRONG.
AT THE END OF THE DAY, HE IS YOUR FATHER. HE NEVER MISTREATED YOU OR LEFT YOU OUT IN THE COLD. SO DO THE SAME FOR HIM.
MM HMM, I GUESS YOU'RE RIGHT.
BUT WHAT ABOUT THE CREDIT CARDS?
THE FORECLOSURE?
THE LIES?

I HEARD FROM JIMMY B., MY FATHER'S HAM RADIO FRIEND, ON THE DAY HE RECEIVED MY LETTER.

HI. WHAT'S UP?

AS YOU KNOW, MY FATHER AND I AREN'T SPEAKING. WELL, RECENTLY, IT'S BECOME REALLY IMPORTANT TO ME TO FIND OUT CERTAIN THINGS.

DOES HE HAVE ACCESS TO YOUR SOCIAL SECURITY NUMBER, BANK ACCOUNT NUMBERS, STUFF LIKE THAT?

SURE, I TRUST HIM TOTALLY.

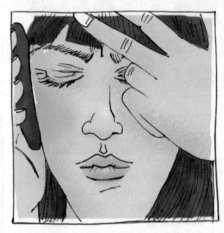

DAYS AFTER THIS CONVERSATION, I RECEIVED AN E-MAIL FROM MARCUS KIPPLINGER, MY FATHER'S FIRST COUSIN WHO WORKED AS AN AP REPORTER IN WASHINGTON, D.C.

YOUR LETTER CAME AS QUITE A PLEASANT SURPRISE. TO GET TO YOUR QUESTION RIGHT AWAY, YOUR FATHER'S FATHER AND MY MOTHER WERE BROTHER AND SISTER. I LAST SAW YOUR DAD IN THE LATE 1950s OR EARLY 1960s.

LATER, WE CONNECTED ON THE PHONE.

SO, ARE YOU STILL IN TOUCH WITH ANYONE IN THE FAMILY?

JUST ELSA, REALLY. SHE LIVES IN BUENOS AIRES.

BINGO! MY FATHER'S HATED STEPSISTER!

I GOT AN IDEA ON THE SPOT.

YOU KNOW, I'D LOVE TO MEET HER. I'M PLANNING TO TRAVEL TO ARGENTINA THIS SUMMER.

SHE'S NOT IN THE BEST OF HEALTH. BUT I COULD CALL HER, I SUPPOSE.

MARCUS CALLED ME AGAIN TWO WEEKS LATER — JUST WHEN I WAS BEGINNING TO THINK ALL WAS LOST.

I'VE SPOKEN TO ELSA, AND SHE'S WILLING TO MEET YOU FOR COFFEE.

GREAT!

A FEW NIGHTS LATER . . .

RING! RING!

149

THE MAN'S VOICE WAS DEEP, ALMOST COMICALLY ITALIAN AMERICAN, LIKE A CHARACTER IN A GANGSTER FILM.

IS THIS THE DAUGHTER OF BILL SANDELL?

DID YOU SEND A LETTER TO GIULIA RUSSO?

YES.

GIULIA— MY FATHER'S SECRETARY! RUSSO MUST HAVE BEEN HER MARRIED NAME!

YES! I'VE BEEN WAITING TO HEAR FROM HER.

THE RUSSOS DON'T WANT NOTHIN' TO DO WITH NO SANDELLS.

CAN I ASK WHO THIS IS?

I WORK FOR GIULIA'S FATHER. I HAD SOME BUSINESS WITH YOUR FATHER ONCE. THAT'S ALL YOU NEED TO KNOW.

ARE YOU STILL IN TOUCH WITH HIM?

NO, HE DROPPED OFF THE RADAR.

IS YOUR FATHER STILL IN THE COUNTRY?

150

I DON'T KNOW. I HAVEN'T HAD CONTACT WITH HIM IN THREE YEARS.

WHAT ABOUT YOUR MOTHER?

LOOK, WHATEVER MY FATHER DID, I'M SURE MY MOTHER HAD NOTHING TO DO WITH IT

YOUR MOTHER KNOWS EVERYTHING.

PLEASE JUST LET GIULIA KNOW I DON'T SPEAK TO MY FATHER, AND IF SHE EVER WANTS TO SAY HELLO, I'D LOVE TO TALK TO HER.

YOU CAN FORGET ABOUT THAT.

DIAL TONE

THE MINUTE I GOT OFF THE PHONE, I CALLED AL.

THAT'S GOTTA BE THE HUSBAND. IF HE KNOWS THAT MUCH, YOUR FATHER SCREWED GIULIA LIKE HE SCREWED THE OTHERS. IT CAN'T BE A JILTING SITUATION, BECAUSE YOUR FATHER WAS MARRIED. SO IF SHE WAS FOOLING AROUND WITH HIM, SHE KNEW IT WAS POTLUCK.

SO WHAT DO YOU THINK HE *DID*?

151

MAYBE HE APPLIED FOR A CREDIT CARD IN HER NAME. SHE THOUGHT SHE WAS WORKING FOR AN HONEST GUY AND FOUND OUT HE WAS A PHONY.

NOW I'LL **NEVER** HEAR FROM HER.

YOU STIRRED UP A LITTLE POT, WHICH IS WHAT WE WANTED TO DO. NOW WE'VE GOT TO MOVE ON.

THAT NIGHT, I HAD TO SIT ON MY HANDS TO NOT CALL BEN. EARLIER I'D FELT SUFFOCATED BY HIS DEPENDABILITY; NOW I WAS CRAVING IT. I DRANK A BOTTLE OF WINE BY MYSELF. I WANTED TO BLACK OUT, AND I DID. I'D DEAL WITH MY FEELINGS IN THE MORNING.

TWO TRUTHS AND A LIE

I HADN'T SEEN MY MOTHER IN MONTHS AND WANTED TO LET HER IN ON SOME OF THE THINGS I'D DISCOVERED. SECRETLY, I WAS HOPING SHE'D HEAR WHAT I HAD TO SAY, BREAK DOWN, AND TELL ME EVERYTHING SHE KNEW. AT THAT POINT, I WASN'T GOING TO GET THE TRUTH — OR ANYTHING CLOSE TO IT — OUT OF MY FATHER. WHICH MEANT IT HAD TO COME FROM HER.

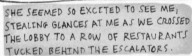

153

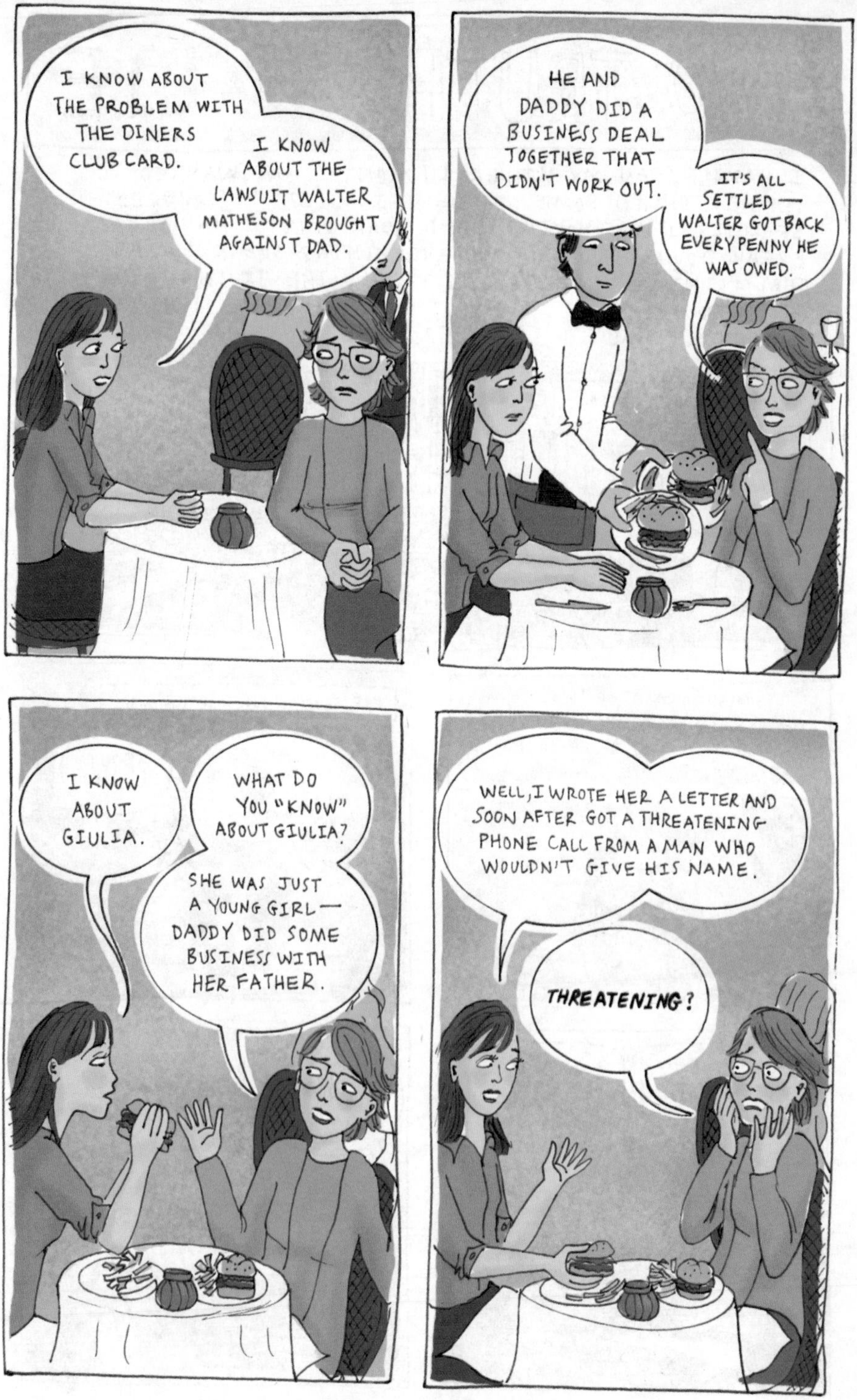
I KNOW ABOUT THE PROBLEM WITH THE DINERS CLUB CARD.
I KNOW ABOUT THE LAWSUIT WALTER MATHESON BROUGHT AGAINST DAD.
HE AND DADDY DID A BUSINESS DEAL TOGETHER THAT DIDN'T WORK OUT.
IT'S ALL SETTLED — WALTER GOT BACK EVERY PENNY HE WAS OWED.
I KNOW ABOUT GIULIA.
WHAT DO YOU "KNOW" ABOUT GIULIA?
SHE WAS JUST A YOUNG GIRL — DADDY DID SOME BUSINESS WITH HER FATHER.
WELL, I WROTE HER A LETTER AND SOON AFTER GOT A THREATENING PHONE CALL FROM A MAN WHO WOULDN'T GIVE HIS NAME.
THREATENING?

HE SAID YOU KNEW EVERYTHING, AND I SHOULD ASK YOU WHAT HAPPENED BETWEEN DAD AND GIULIA.

I KNOW YOU THINK I'M TOTALLY NAIVE, BUT I'M NOT. I SEE WHAT GOES ON.... I CHOOSE TO GIVE DADDY THE BENEFIT OF THE DOUBT.

BUT THE EVIDENCE IS MOUNTING, MOM. DAD SEEMS TO BE DOING ILLEGAL THINGS. ARE YOU WILLING TO GIVE HIM THE BENEFIT OF THE DOUBT WHEN THERE IS *SO MUCH* DOUBT?

WELL, *I DON'T DOUBT HIM!*

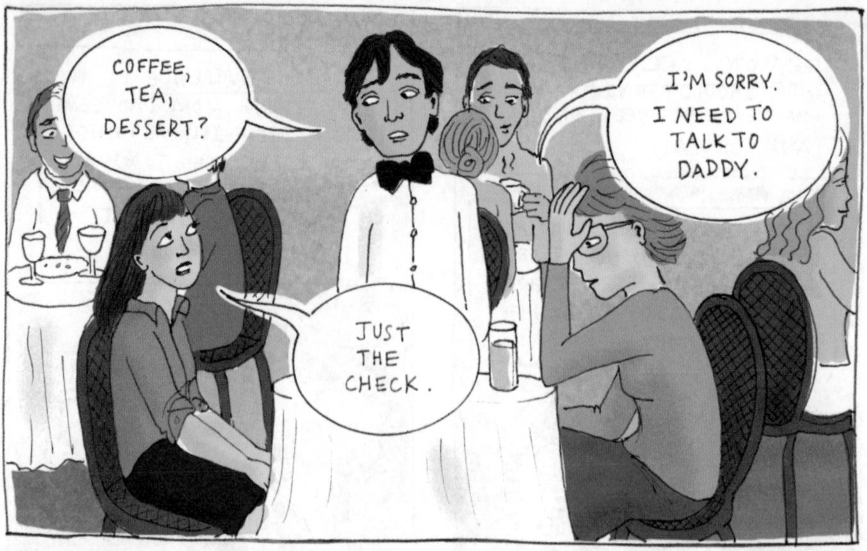
COFFEE, TEA, DESSERT?
I'M SORRY. I NEED TO TALK TO DADDY.
JUST THE CHECK.

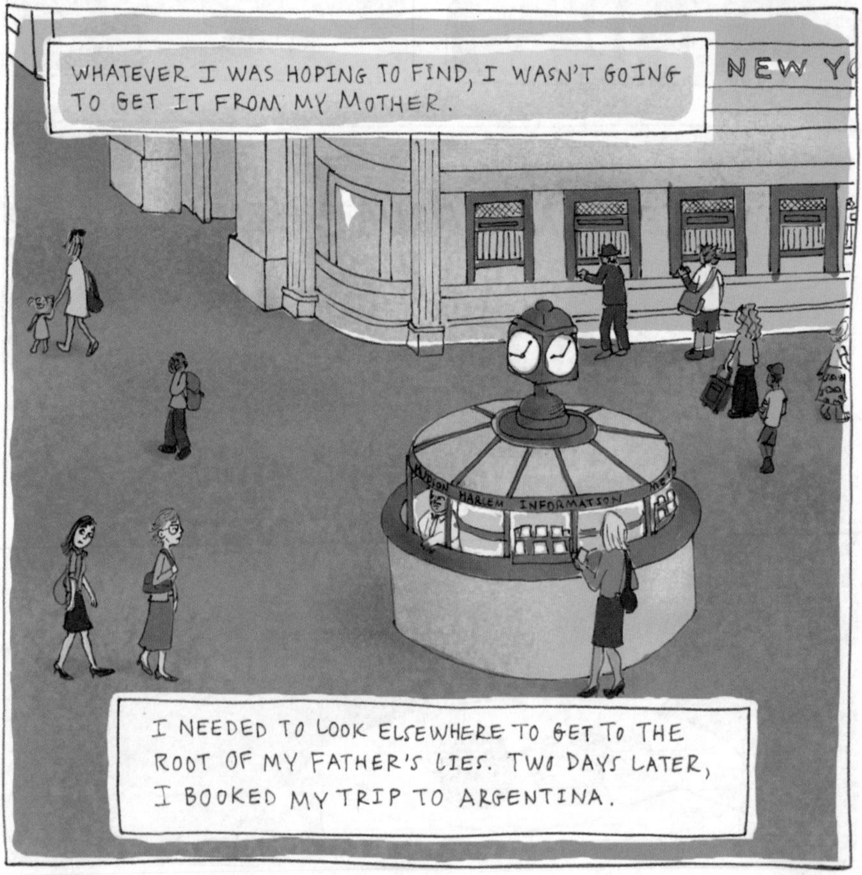
WHATEVER I WAS HOPING TO FIND, I WASN'T GOING TO GET IT FROM MY MOTHER.
NEW YO
HARLEM
INFORMATION
I NEEDED TO LOOK ELSEWHERE TO GET TO THE ROOT OF MY FATHER'S LIES. TWO DAYS LATER, I BOOKED MY TRIP TO ARGENTINA.

ARGENTINA

I ARRIVED IN BUENOS AIRES WITH TWO OBJECTIVES: (1) SEE THE CITY WHERE MY FATHER WAS BORN; (2) MEET ELSA. I HAD HER PHONE NUMBER IN MY POCKET. IT WAS THE OFF-SEASON IN ARGENTINA. THE NIGHT I CHECKED IN, I WAS THE ONLY PERSON IN THE HOTEL. MALABIA HOUSE WAS BEAUTIFUL AND **CHEAP**.

AUGUST 2006

POWER OF THE DOLLAR

WITHIN TWENTY MINUTES, I'D UNPACKED MY BACKPACK, PLACED MY BALLED-UP SOCKS IN A DRAWER, AND HUNG MY T-SHIRTS ON HANGERS. THEN I PASSED OUT.

A FEW HOURS LATER, I HEADED OUTSIDE TO FIND DINNER.

157

WAS I IMAGINING IT, OR DID THE WOMEN IN THIS COUNTRY **LOOK** LIKE ME?

LATER THAT NIGHT...

I NEED SOME INFO ON GRANDPA'S GRAVE. I'M ALREADY IN ARGENTINA — WHY HAVEN'T YOU RESPONDED?

WHEN I REFRESHED MY BROWSER, I FOUND AN E-MAIL FROM BEN, TELLING ME HOW MUCH HE MISSED ME. HE SAID HE'D FINALLY GOTTEN FINANCING TO DIRECT A MOVIE HE'D WRITTEN, STARRING SOME OF THE BIGGEST NAMES IN HOLLYWOOD.

JUST SEEING HIS E-MAIL ADDRESS IN MY INBOX — SO FAMILIAR — INSTANTLY COMFORTED ME.

I WROTE BACK TO HIM RIGHT AWAY. I CONGRATULATED HIM AND DESCRIBED MY TRIP SO FAR.

THEN I CLICKED "SEND" AND STRETCHED OUT ON THE DIVAN, LISTENING TO THE HUM OF THE OVERHEAD LIGHT. NOW WHAT?

WHEN I WOKE UP, IT WAS LIGHT OUTSIDE. I DECIDED TO GO TO THE UNIVERSITY OF BUENOS AIRES TO LOOK UP MY FATHER'S RECORDS. NONE OF THE UNIVERSITIES HE'D CLAIMED TO HAVE ATTENDED HAD PANNED OUT. BUT HE HAD TO HAVE STUDIED **SOMEWHERE.**

MALABIA HOUSE OFFERED TO SET ME UP WITH A TRANSLATOR. RAYEN MET ME IN THE BREAKFAST ROOM WITH HER BOYFRIEND, JOE.

WE SET OUT FOR THE UBA CAMPUS.

WOW, THIS IS LIKE SOMETHING OUT OF A GRAHAM GREENE NOVEL!

OFICINA DE REGISTROS

SHE SAYS ALL THE RECORDS ARE HERE, BUT SHE CAN ONLY SHOW THEM TO THE PEOPLE THEY BELONG TO.

TEN MINUTES LATER . . .

THERE'S NO RECORD OF YOUR FATHER. SHE CHECKED ALL THE WAY BACK TO THE FIFTIES.

I WAS DISAPPOINTED AND, FRANKLY, IMPRESSED. HOW HAD HE TAUGHT COLLEGE-LEVEL ECONOMICS WITHOUT AN EDUCATION?

THAT AFTERNOON, I CALLED MY FATHER'S STEPSISTER, ELSA.

ALO?

ELSA?

WE MADE A PLAN TO MEET LATER IN THE WEEK.

160

I SPENT THE NEXT FEW DAYS OF MY TRIP SIGHTSEEING.

I SAW THE PINK HOUSE.

CLICK!

I WATCHED A TANGO PERFORMANCE.

CLAP CLAP CLAP

I STROLLED THROUGH THE MARKET OF SAN TELMO.

EVERYWHERE I LOOKED, I SAW SIGNS OF MY FATHER.

CARLOS GARDEL

161

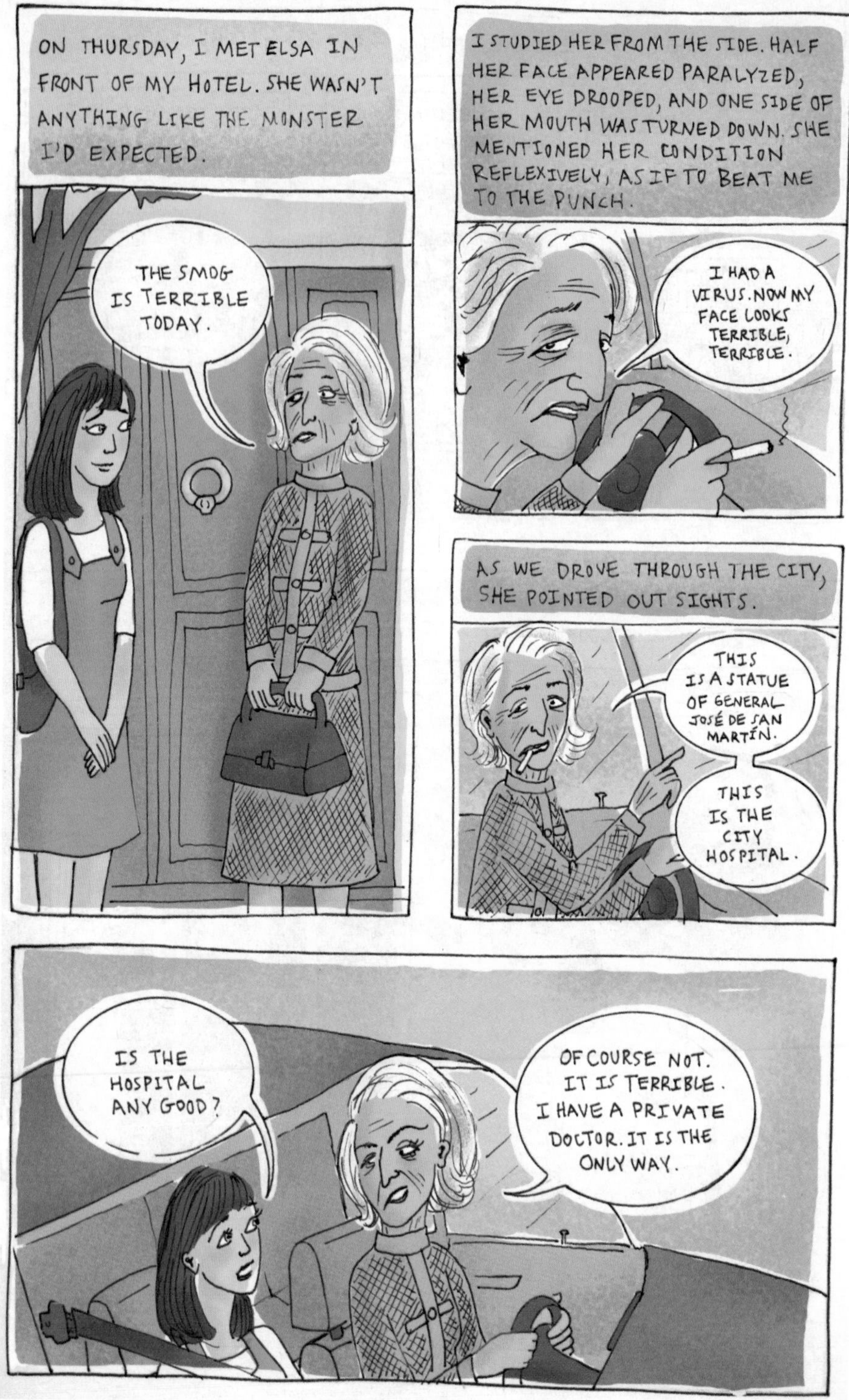
ON THURSDAY, I MET ELSA IN FRONT OF MY HOTEL. SHE WASN'T ANYTHING LIKE THE MONSTER I'D EXPECTED.
THE SMOG IS TERRIBLE TODAY.
I STUDIED HER FROM THE SIDE. HALF HER FACE APPEARED PARALYZED, HER EYE DROOPED, AND ONE SIDE OF HER MOUTH WAS TURNED DOWN. SHE MENTIONED HER CONDITION REFLEXIVELY, AS IF TO BEAT ME TO THE PUNCH.
I HAD A VIRUS. NOW MY FACE LOOKS TERRIBLE, TERRIBLE.
AS WE DROVE THROUGH THE CITY, SHE POINTED OUT SIGHTS.
THIS IS A STATUE OF GENERAL JOSÉ DE SAN MARTÍN.
THIS IS THE CITY HOSPITAL.
IS THE HOSPITAL ANY GOOD?
OF COURSE NOT. IT IS TERRIBLE. I HAVE A PRIVATE DOCTOR. IT IS THE ONLY WAY.

SHE TOLD ME ABOUT HER CHILD-HOOD IN VIENNA AND THE GATED COMMUNITY IN BUENOS AIRES SHE'D GROWN UP IN AFTER MY GRANDFATHER MARRIED HER MOTHER.

WE CAN HAVE LUNCH AT THE CLUB.

HER ENTITLED HAUTEUR GAVE ME INSIGHT: SHE HAD GOTTEN TOO MUCH AND MY FATHER TOO LITTLE.

SO YOU GREW UP WITH MY FATHER, RIGHT?

HE HAD HIS LIFE, AND I HAD MINE.

I WAS JUST WONDERING. WE DON'T SPEAK.

OH, REALLY? THAT'S TOO BAD.

SHE QUICKLY CHANGED THE SUBJECT.

THERE'S THE FOOTBALL STADIUM. AH, AND THERE'S THE CLUB.

163

SHE LED ME TO THE DINING ROOM, WITH ITS HIGH CEILINGS AND ENORMOUS ROUND TABLES, AND WE SAT BY A WINDOW, OVERLOOKING AN EXPANSIVE GREEN LAWN.

A COURSE FOR THE HORSES.

OK, BUT I USUALLY DON'T. NO ONE SMOKES IN THE STATES ANYMORE.

ACH— I AM STILL HERE!

OVER LUNCH, WE MADE LIGHT CONVERSATION ABOUT OUR LIVES.

SO WHERE DO YOU LIVE?

IN A VERY NICE NEIGHBORHOOD.

ALONE?

WITH MY SON, MANUEL.

THE SMALL TALK WAS EXCRUCIATING. I WAS CIRCLING AROUND THE QUESTIONS I REALLY WANTED TO ASK. SHE WAS THE ONLY PERSON I KNEW WHO'D KNOWN MY FATHER BEFORE ALL THE LIES.

WHAT WAS MY FATHER LIKE AS A CHILD?

WHAT DOES HE DO?

OH, HE'LL BE FINISHING SCHOOL FOR THE REST OF HIS LIFE.

WHY DOES HE HATE YOU SO MUCH?

WHY ALL THE LIES?

WAS HE EVER DIFFERENT?

MY FATHER DESCRIBED HIS FATHER AS EXTREMELY BRILLIANT AND CONNECTED. IS THAT TRUE?

YES, YES — HE WAS EXTREMELY EDUCATED.

DO YOU HAPPEN TO KNOW WHY MY FATHER LEFT ARGENTINA?

YES, I DO.

STUB STUB STUB

HE DESERTED THE ARMY. THEY CAME LOOKING FOR HIM. A VERY NICE OFFICER ASKED MY FATHER IF YOUR FATHER WAS HIDING IN THE HOUSE. HE WASN'T ANYWHERE TO BE FOUND. HE LATER CALLED, AND MY FATHER GOT HIM OUT OF THE COUNTRY, INTO PARAGUAY.

THAT'S ALL I KNOW — AND THAT'S ALL I **WANT** TO KNOW.

ALL THE WOMEN IN MY FATHER'S LIFE SEEMED TO CLOSE THEIR EYES.

BUT I NEED TO KNOW A BIT MORE. FOR EXAMPLE, HE HAS ALL THESE UNIVERSITY DEGREES, AND I CAN'T FIND EVIDENCE OF ANY OF THEM.

HE NEVER WENT TO ANY UNIVERSITY. I THINK HE GRADUATED HIGH SCHOOL.

BUT HIS EDUCATION HAD TO COME FROM SOMEWHERE —

IT WAS A REALLY GOOD CATHOLIC BOARDING SCHOOL, RIGHT?

BOARDING SCHOOL? NO.

DO YOU REMEMBER WHICH SCHOOL HE WENT TO?

THE ONLY ONE THAT WOULD TAKE HIM!

AT THAT, I TOLD HER ABOUT MY CONVERSATION WITH THE DEAN OF THE COMMUNITY COLLEGE AND HOW I'D FOUND OUT MY FATHER'S CREDENTIALS WERE FORGED.

I WOULD HAVE HOPED HE HAD CHANGED BY NOW.

166

SO DID YOU GROW UP WITH MY FATHER?

NO, YOUR FATHER LIVED WITH HIS MOTHER.

SHE WAS WILD. ALWAYS A DIFFERENT MAN. SHE ASKED MY FATHER FOR MONEY ALL THE TIME. HE GAVE IT TO HER JUST TO MAKE HER GO AWAY.

WOW.

"SOMETIMES MY FATHER WOULD TAKE THE BOY FOR A FEW DAYS, AND HIS MOTHER NEVER SHOWED UP TO GET HIM."

HAVE YOU EVER MET HER?

ONLY IN THE LAST YEAR OF HER LIFE. THEY WERE ESTRANGED UNTIL THEN.

SO WHEN IS THE LAST TIME YOU SAW MY FATHER?

AFTER MY FATHER DIED.

HE COMMITTED SUICIDE, YOU KNOW.

YES, I KNOW.

RIGHT AFTERWARD, YOUR FATHER CAME TO ARGENTINA AND TRIED TO GET MONEY FROM ME.

SERIOUSLY?

MY FATHER OWNED A FACTORY THAT WAS DOING VERY WELL. BUT YOUR FATHER COULDN'T TOUCH THE MONEY. BECAUSE EARLIER, HE HAD CLEANED OUT A BANK ACCOUNT OF MY FATHER'S.

WHEN?

I DON'T KNOW; WHEN HE WAS YOUNGER. IT BROKE MY FATHER'S HEART.

THERE WERE RARE TIMES WHEN THE EMOTION MY FATHER SHOWED SEEMED GENUINE; ONE OF THEM WAS WHEN HE TALKED ABOUT HIS FATHER. SO I FOUND THIS NEWS SHOCKING.

"THE MINUTE YOUR FATHER HEARD ABOUT HIS FATHER'S DEATH, HE CAME TO ARGENTINA."

SELL THE FACTORY AND GIVE ME MY HALF!

ABSOLUTELY NOT.

"I HAD A BRIEFCASE FULL OF PAPERS IN THE LIVING ROOM. I WENT INTO THE OTHER ROOM, AND WHEN I RETURNED, THE BRIEFCASE WAS GONE, AND SO WAS HE."

"BUT HE TOOK THE WRONG ONE! I'D ALREADY GIVEN THE *REAL* BRIEF-CASE — WITH THE PAPERS THAT PROVED OWNERSHIP OF THE FAC-TORY — TO MY HUSBAND TO HIDE, BECAUSE I THOUGHT HE MIGHT TRY SOMETHING LIKE THAT."

I NEVER SAW HIM AGAIN.

IF HE RANG MY DOORBELL TODAY, I WOULDN'T LET HIM IN.

I FELT A SUDDEN URGE TO PROTECT MY FATHER FROM THIS WOMAN WHO CLEARLY HATED HIM. BUT THE DRIVE TO PRESS ON WAS STRONGER.

DO YOU HAPPEN TO KNOW WHY HE CHANGED HIS NAME? BECAUSE MY LAST NAME IS SANDELL.

SOMETHING TO DO WITH A BANK HE WAS WORKING FOR IN NEW YORK.

HE'S BEEN RUNNING FROM "SCHMIDT" EVER SINCE.

169

DO YOU OWN A LOT OF ART?

OH, YES. I HAVE SOME OF HIS AND SOME OF HIS TOO.

I DON'T HAVE THE WALL SPACE FOR IT ALL. I WILL HAVE TO SELL SOME.

BACK AT THE HOTEL . . .

I KNEW I SHOULDN'T CALL BEN, GIVEN MY HISTORY OF AMBIVALENCE ABOUT HIM.

BUT I WAS LONELY IN THAT NEARLY EMPTY HOTEL, MY ONLY COMPANY THE OCCASIONAL SOUND OF A MAID'S FOOTSTEPS.

SO WHAT HAS FILMING BEEN LIKE?

FORGET ABOUT THAT — I WANT TO HEAR ABOUT ELSA!

170

WE TALKED FOR HOURS. IT FELT SO GOOD TO HAVE SOMEONE TO SHARE ALL THIS WITH. AND NOT JUST SOMEONE — **BEN.**

YOU'RE KIDDING! SHE ACTUALLY **SAID** THAT?

FOR MONTHS I'D FELT UNMOORED, ADRIFT.

GOD, I CAN'T BELIEVE YOU'VE BEEN HAVING SUCH CRAZY ADVENTURES.

UNSEEN.

TELL ME MORE. I CAN'T GET ENOUGH!

BY THE END OF THE NIGHT, I FELT LIKE I EXISTED AGAIN.

THE NEXT DAY, I HIRED A DRIVER TO TAKE ME TO MEMORIAL CEMETERY, WHERE MY GRANDFATHER WAS BURIED. IT LOOKED LIKE A COUNTRY CLUB.

A BLONDE WOMAN DROVE ME OUT TO THE PLOT IN A LITTLE GOLF CART.

SHE STOOD RESPECTFULLY TO ONE SIDE AS I SNAPPED A PICTURE.

AFTERWARD, I HAD THE DRIVER TAKE ME TO RECOLETA, ONE OF THE WEALTHIEST NEIGHBORHOODS IN BUENOS AIRES, TO LOOK AT MY GRANDFATHER'S FORMER HOME.

THEN WE DROVE TO ELSA'S APARTMENT. THE NEIGHBORHOOD WAS EQUALLY POSH. TOO NERVOUS TO GET OUT OF THE CAR, I ROLLED DOWN THE WINDOW AND SNAPPED A PICTURE FROM THE FRONT SEAT.

ALL I SAW, WHEN I LOOKED AT THE HOUSE, WAS EVERYTHING MY FATHER HAD BEEN DENIED. IT WAS A HOUSE — AND A LIFE — THAT MADE HIM PRETEND TO BE EVERYTHING HE WASN'T.

Contract of Denial

A FEW DAYS AFTER I RETURNED TO NEW YORK, I GOT A PHONE CALL FROM MY MOTHER.

WHY ARE YOU WHISPERING?

I'M IN THE BACKYARD— SO DADDY WON'T HEAR.

I COULD HEAR HER FUMBLING WITH A PIECE OF PAPER.

I WROTE A FEW THINGS DOWN, SO I COULD REMEMBER WHAT I WANTED TO SAY.

I KNOW YOU WENT TO ARGENTINA.

IT'S TRUE.

I KNOW YOU MET ELSA.

ALSO TRUE.

SHE STARTED TO CRY.

SOME PEOPLE LIKE TO SPILL THEIR GUTS.

I'M NOT LIKE THAT. I'M MORE OF A PRIVATE PERSON.

I KNOW YOU ARE, BUT—

I THINK PARENTS HAVE THE RIGHT TO TAKE CERTAIN THINGS TO THE GRAVE.

I RESPECT THAT, MOM. BUT THE THINGS YOU'RE REFERRING TO AFFECTED ME DIRECTLY. SO PRIVACY ISN'T THE ISSUE HERE.

YOUR FIRST LOYALTY SHOULD BE TO THE FAMILY.

174

IT WAS A REFRAIN. SOMETHING MY MOTHER HAD BEEN SAYING SINCE I WAS A KID. BUT THIS LOYALTY HAD COST ME DEARLY. FOR IT, I'D SACRIFICED SO MANY THINGS: TRUST IN MEN. MY ABILITY TO LOVE. A CLEAN CREDIT REPORT. MY VERY SENSE OF SELF. THE TRUTH WAS MORE IMPORTANT THAN LOYALTY.

I DON'T WANT YOU TO RUIN MY LIFE.

RUIN YOUR LIFE?

BECAUSE I HAVE A CHILD WHO'S GOING TO EXPOSE MY LIFE, AND I DON'T THINK I'M STRONG ENOUGH TO JUST WALK AWAY FROM MY HUSBAND.

WHO IS ASKING YOU TO WALK AWAY?

LAURIE... JUST STOP.

I CAN'T STOP.

175

The Price of Fiction

MY MOTHER ARRANGED A MEETING. SHE PICKED ME UP AT THE TRAIN STATION AND DROVE ME TO MY PARENTS' HOUSE. NEITHER OF US SAID MUCH ON THE DRIVE THERE.

OH! I MISSED THE TURN.

WHEN I WALKED INTO THE HOUSE, I SAW MY FATHER STANDING IN THE LIVING ROOM.

IT'S BEEN A LONG TIME, LAURIE. THREE AND A HALF YEARS.

TEARS WELLED, BUT I BLINKED THEM BACK. I WAS DETERMINED TO HOLD ON TO MY HARD-WON STOICISM.

YES, IT HAS.

MY FATHER LOOKED DIFFERENT. ONE SIDE OF HIS MUSTACHE WAS LONGER THAN THE OTHER, AND HE WAS HEAVIER THAN USUAL.

AH... WHY DON'T YOU SIT THERE?

OOF.

FOR A FEW MINUTES, HE SAID NOTHING.

THEN...

EVERYONE KNOWS ABOUT THE DEGREES. I WAS AT A FAMILY PARTY AND FOUND OUT YOU'D SPOKEN TO AUNT OLIVE. YOU'D SPOKEN TO COUSIN LISA. YOU'D SPOKEN TO BOTH OF YOUR SISTERS. AND YOU'D TOLD COUSIN ROSE, WHO TOLD HER HUSBAND, DAN, AND, STUPID ASSHOLE THAT HE WAS, HE TOLD THE REST OF THE FAMILY. I WAS THE LAST TO KNOW.

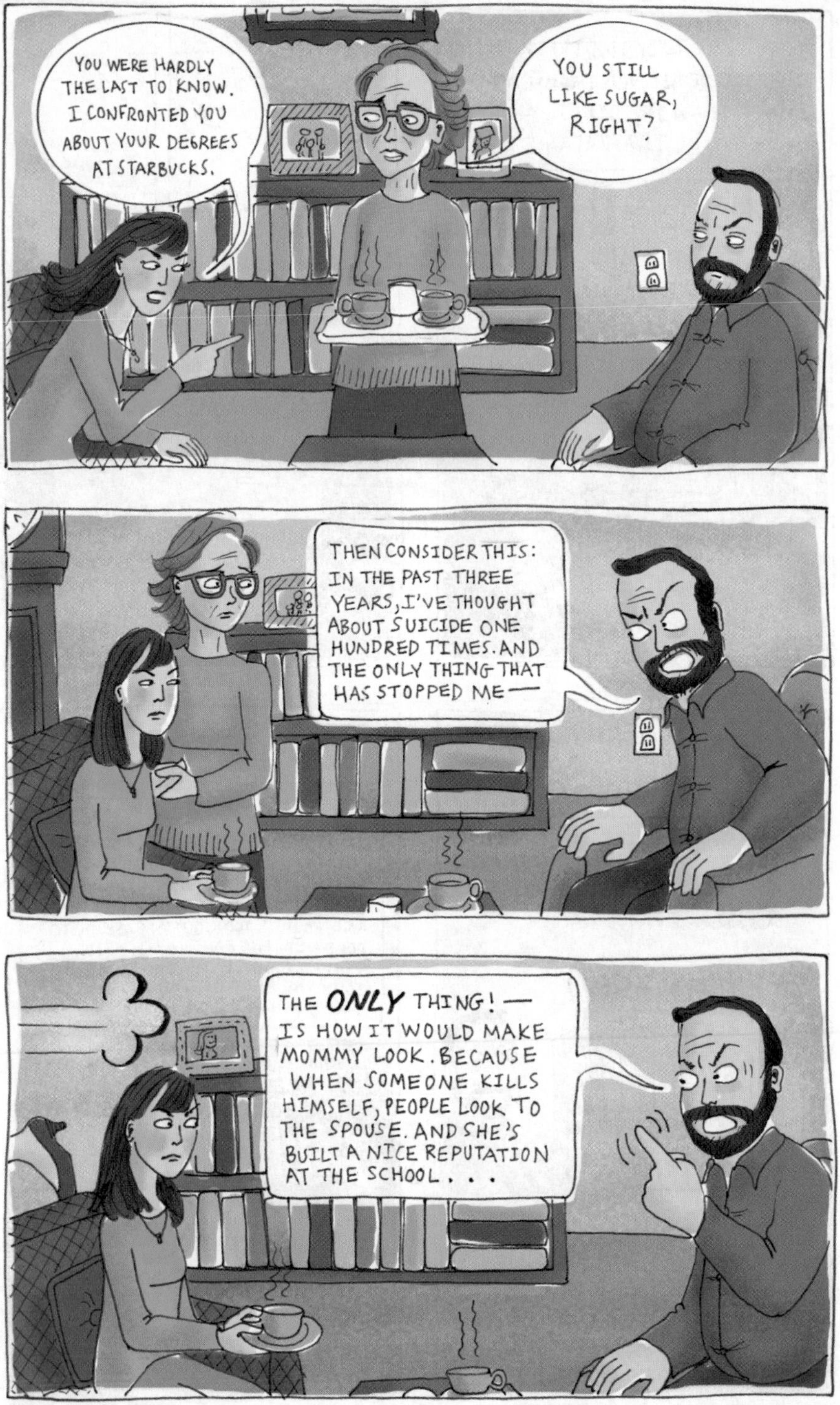
YOU WERE HARDLY THE LAST TO KNOW. I CONFRONTED YOU ABOUT YOUR DEGREES AT STARBUCKS.
YOU STILL LIKE SUGAR, RIGHT?
THEN CONSIDER THIS: IN THE PAST THREE YEARS, I'VE THOUGHT ABOUT SUICIDE ONE HUNDRED TIMES. AND THE ONLY THING THAT HAS STOPPED ME—
THE ONLY THING! — IS HOW IT WOULD MAKE MOMMY LOOK. BECAUSE WHEN SOMEONE KILLS HIMSELF, PEOPLE LOOK TO THE SPOUSE. AND SHE'S BUILT A NICE REPUTATION AT THE SCHOOL . . .

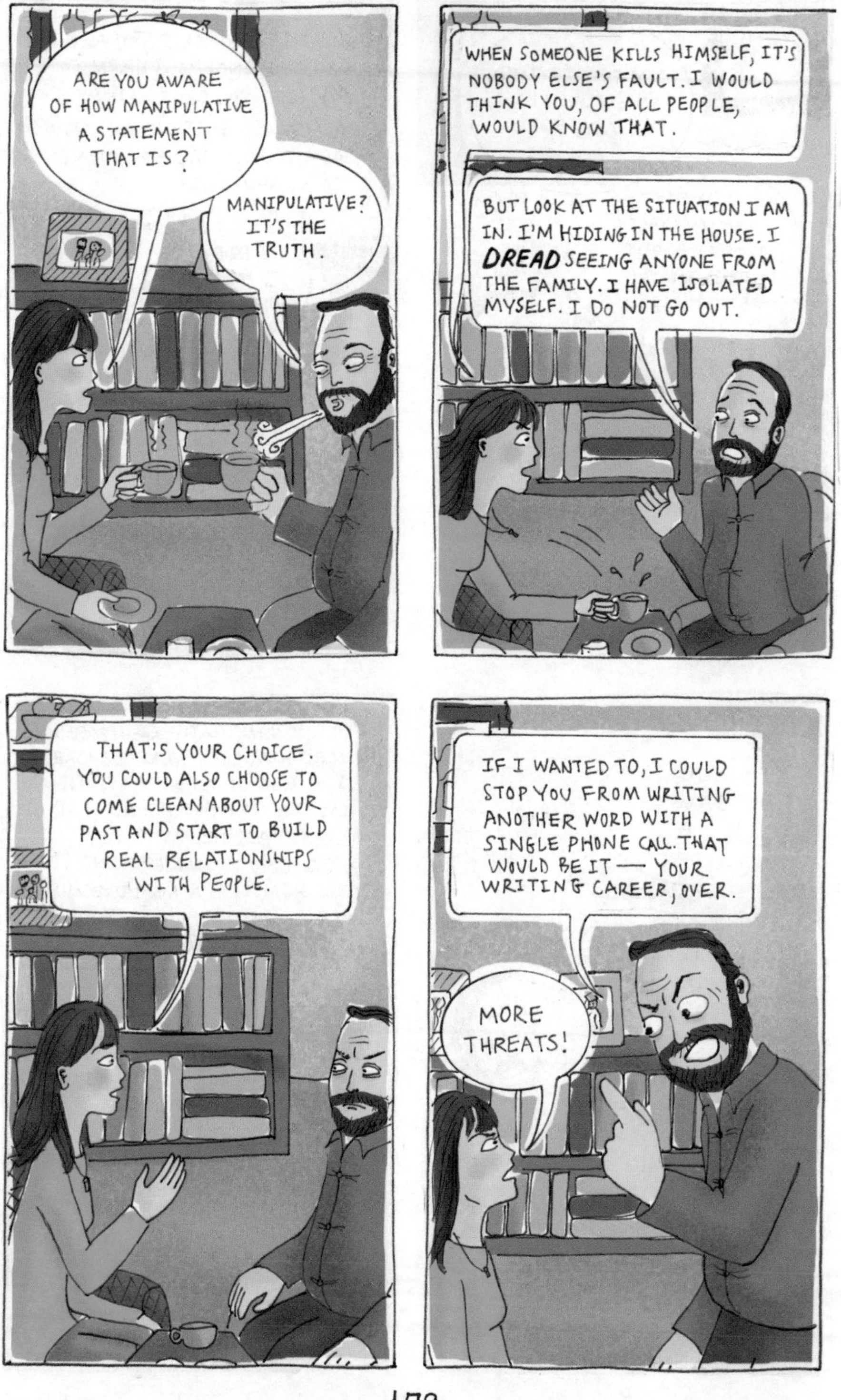
ARE YOU AWARE OF HOW MANIPULATIVE A STATEMENT THAT IS?
MANIPULATIVE? IT'S THE TRUTH.
WHEN SOMEONE KILLS HIMSELF, IT'S NOBODY ELSE'S FAULT. I WOULD THINK YOU, OF ALL PEOPLE, WOULD KNOW THAT.
BUT LOOK AT THE SITUATION I AM IN. I'M HIDING IN THE HOUSE. I DREAD SEEING ANYONE FROM THE FAMILY. I HAVE ISOLATED MYSELF. I DO NOT GO OUT.
THAT'S YOUR CHOICE. YOU COULD ALSO CHOOSE TO COME CLEAN ABOUT YOUR PAST AND START TO BUILD REAL RELATIONSHIPS WITH PEOPLE.
IF I WANTED TO, I COULD STOP YOU FROM WRITING ANOTHER WORD WITH A SINGLE PHONE CALL. THAT WOULD BE IT — YOUR WRITING CAREER, OVER.
MORE THREATS!

I'M JUST TRYING TO EXPLAIN HOW LOYALTY WORKS.

THIS ISN'T ABOUT LOYALTY. THIS IS ABOUT TELLING THE TRUTH ABOUT MY LIFE.

BUT IN THE PROCESS, YOU ARE CAUSING ENORMOUS HARM TO **MY** LIFE. YOU CALLED JIMMY B. YOU CALLED GUSTAVO. AND NOW MOMMY TELLS ME YOU WENT TO ARGENTINA!

I DID. I MET WITH ELSA.

YOU SAW ELSA?

YES.

YOU KNOW MY FATHER SUPPOSEDLY KILLED HIMSELF? WELL, I SPOKE WITH A MAN WHO WAS WITH HIM THE DAY BEFORE HE DIED, AND HE SAID HE WAS HAPPY AND IN NO FRAME OF MIND TO KILL HIMSELF. A MAN DOESN'T TAKE PILLS THE DAY AFTER HE IS FEELING FINE.

SO WHAT ARE YOU SAYING — THAT ELSA AND HER MOTHER POISONED HIM?

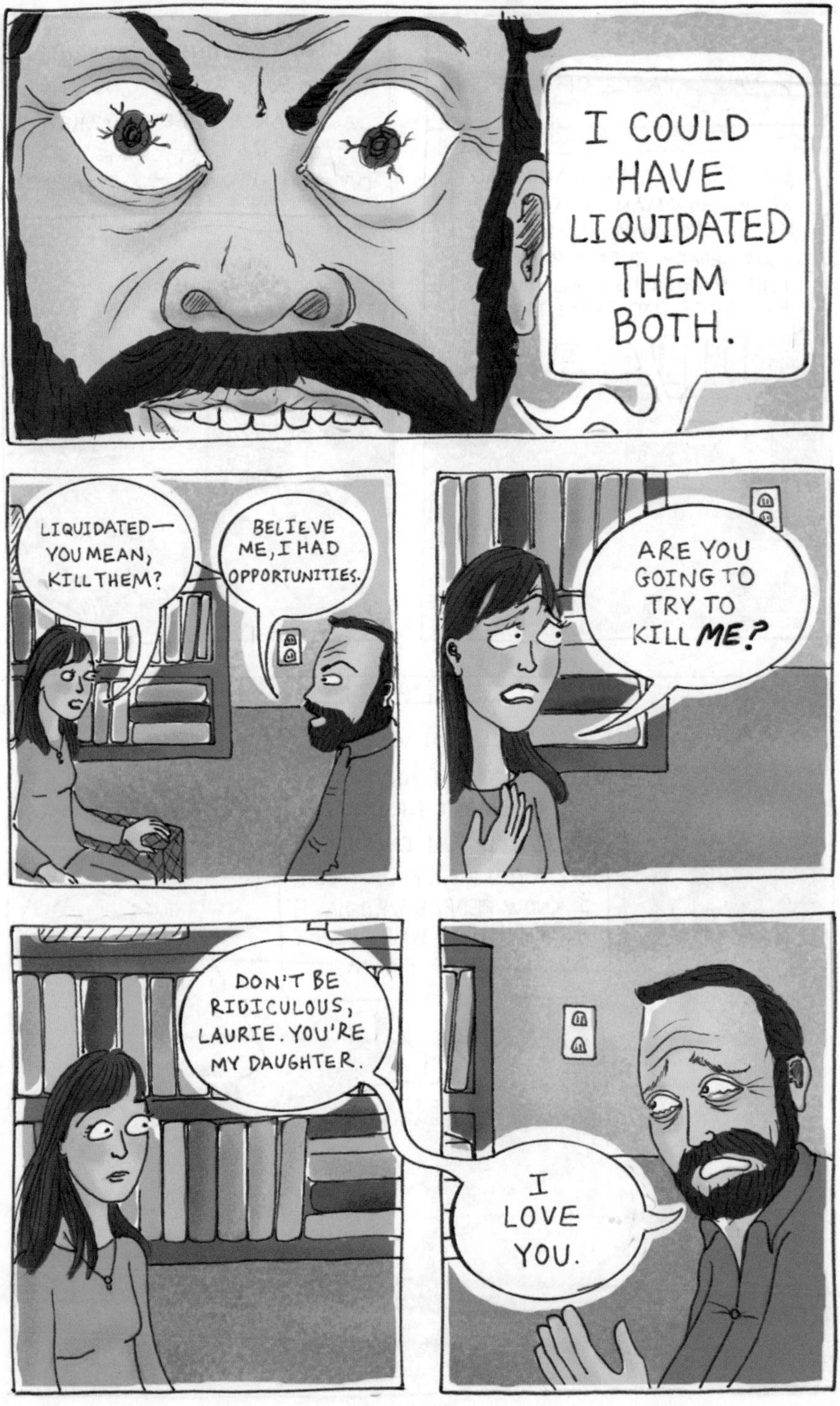
I COULD HAVE LIQUIDATED THEM BOTH.
LIQUIDATED— YOU MEAN, KILL THEM?
BELIEVE ME, I HAD OPPORTUNITIES.
ARE YOU GOING TO TRY TO KILL ***ME?***
DON'T BE RIDICULOUS, LAURIE. YOU'RE MY DAUGHTER.
I LOVE YOU.

I STILL WANTED TO BELIEVE HE WAS CAPABLE OF LOVE.

LIFE IS SHORT, DAD, AND WHO KNOWS HOW MANY YEARS YOU HAVE LEFT. DO YOU REALLY WANT YOUR LEGACY TO BE A PACK OF LIES, WHEN THE REAL YOU IS FAR MORE INTERESTING?

THIS WAS IT: ONE LAST CHANCE TO LET GO OF HIS FICTIONS. ONE LAST CHANCE TO BE A FATHER. I DIDN'T HAVE IT IN ME TO OFFER HIM MORE THAN THAT.

WHY DON'T YOU LET US LOVE *YOU* BY BEING WHO YOU REALLY ARE?

I'LL TELL YOU WHO I REALLY AM: I AM ONE OF THE MOST ERUDITE, EDUCATED, AND CULTURED MEN YOU WILL EVER MEET. I KNOW PEOPLE WHO HAVE *FIVE* PHDs WHO AREN'T AS SMART AS I AM.

SO YOU'D RATHER GO TO THE GRAVE WITH YOUR SECRETS.

WHAT DOES IT MATTER? WHEN I DIE, YOU'LL FORGET ABOUT ME ANYWAY.

ALL FINISHED HERE? LAURIE, WHAT TIME IS YOUR TRAIN?

THE NEXT ONE IS AT EIGHT TWENTY P.M.

YOU'D BETTER TAKE HER NOW.

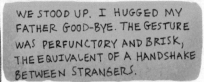

WE STOOD UP. I HUGGED MY FATHER GOOD-BYE. THE GESTURE WAS PERFUNCTORY AND BRISK, THE EQUIVALENT OF A HANDSHAKE BETWEEN STRANGERS.

MY MOTHER DROVE ME TO THE STATION, AND WE SAT IN THE DARK CAR, WAITING FOR MY TRAIN TO ARRIVE.

NOW WE CAN BE A FAMILY AGAIN.

I'M GLAD YOU OUTED HIM, LAURIE.

I WASN'T SURE I'D HEARD HER CORRECTLY: WAS SHE TIRED OF LIVING A LIE TOO? HAD SHE BEEN MORE SUPPORTIVE OF ME THAN ANYONE KNEW?

YOU ARE? WHY?

BECAUSE I DON'T CARE WHO HE IS. I STILL LOVE HIM.

HER LAST WORDS SEEMED TO HANG IN THE AIR. THEY WERE PROOF POSITIVE SHE WAS NEVER GOING TO CHANGE.

Metro-North Railroad

THAT WAS OK. SHE WASN'T THE ONE WHO NEEDED TO.

Metro-North Railroad

Good-bye, DOUBT

I WAS IN TORONTO TO DO AN-OTHER INTERVIEW. WHEN I RETURNED TO MY HOTEL ROOM, I DIALED BEN.

I'M SO GLAD WE TALKED WHEN I WAS IN ARGENTINA. I MISS YOU.

I MISS YOU TOO.

I WANT TO TRY AGAIN.

LAURIE...

IT SEEMED SO CLEAR TO ME. BEN WAS THE ONLY PERSON WHO HAD EVER FULLY ACCEPTED ME. THE ONLY ONE WHO'D SEEMED TO LOVE ME FOR EXACTLY WHO I WAS — EVEN WHEN I WASN'T SURE WHO THAT WAS.

I MEAN IT! I LOVE YOU. IT'S JUST THAT I'VE NEVER BEEN ABLE TO TRUST ANYONE BECAUSE OF MY FUCKED-UP CHILDHOOD.

YOU KNOW I WANT THAT TOO, BUT...

IN THAT MOMENT, I FORGOT ALL MY RESERVATIONS ABOUT BEN. HIS PASSIVITY; HIS REFUSAL TO TALK ABOUT OUR RELATIONSHIP UNLESS WE WERE ON THE VERGE OF BREAKING UP; HIS RELUCTANCE TO BE A DAD; HIS DENIAL ABOUT MY AMBIVALENCE TOWARD HIM. ALL I KNEW WAS THAT I WANTED HIM.

BUT WHAT?

WHERE IS THIS COMING FROM? IS THIS BECAUSE I'M LESS AVAIL-ABLE NOW, WITH THE MOVIE?

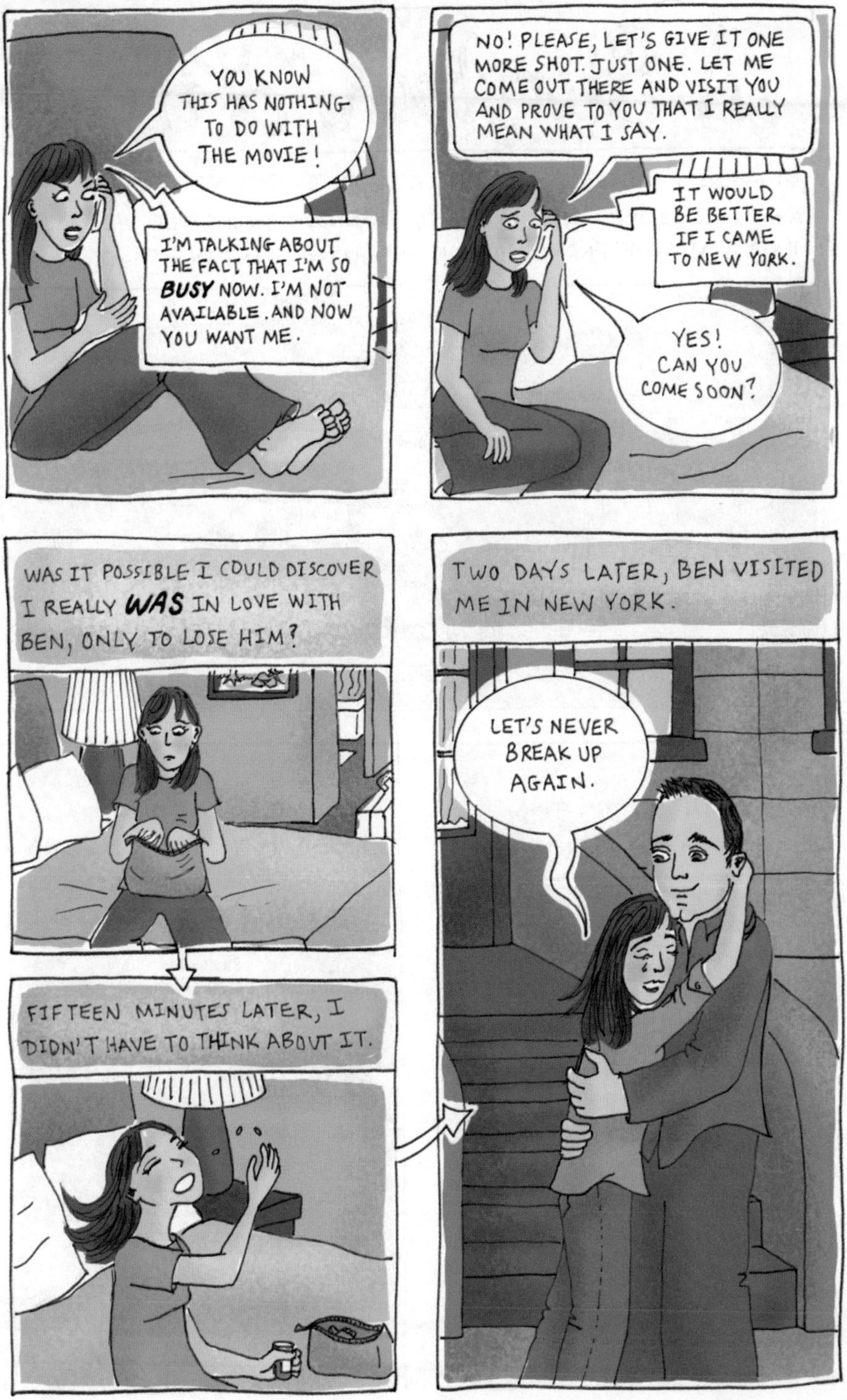
YOU KNOW THIS HAS NOTHING TO DO WITH THE MOVIE!
I'M TALKING ABOUT THE FACT THAT I'M SO **BUSY** NOW. I'M NOT AVAILABLE. AND NOW YOU WANT ME.
NO! PLEASE, LET'S GIVE IT ONE MORE SHOT. JUST ONE. LET ME COME OUT THERE AND VISIT YOU AND PROVE TO YOU THAT I REALLY MEAN WHAT I SAY.
IT WOULD BE BETTER IF I CAME TO NEW YORK.
YES! CAN YOU COME SOON?
WAS IT POSSIBLE I COULD DISCOVER I REALLY **WAS** IN LOVE WITH BEN, ONLY TO LOSE HIM?
FIFTEEN MINUTES LATER, I DIDN'T HAVE TO THINK ABOUT IT.
TWO DAYS LATER, BEN VISITED ME IN NEW YORK.
LET'S NEVER BREAK UP AGAIN.

A Storybook Life

IN APRIL, I WAS SENT TO NASHVILLE TO INTERVIEW ASHLEY JUDD AGAIN. A CAR SERVICE TOOK ME TO FRANKLIN, TENNESSEE. WE PASSED MILES OF FARMLAND, COWS AND HORSES, WINDING ROADS.

WE PULLED UP TO A MASSIVE MANSION SET ON TWO HUNDRED ACRES OF LAND.

I SAT DOWN IN HER SUNROOM: IT WAS FILLED WITH FLORAL COUCHES, GARDENING BOOKS, AND FRAMED FAMILY PORTRAITS.

SHE'LL BE DOWN IN A MINUTE.

FIFTEEN MINUTES LATER, ASHLEY WALKED INTO THE ROOM.

HELLO! DID YOU HAVE A GOOD TRIP? LET'S GO OUTSIDE.

SHE PREPARED TWO BOWLS OF HOMEMADE ICE CREAM AND SPREAD A BLANKET ON THE GRASS. HER DOG AND CAT FROLICKED AROUND US AS WE LAY ON THE BLANKET, LOOKING OVER MILES OF ROLLING GREEN PASTURE.

THOSE ARE MY BLUEBELLS; I PLANTED THEM MYSELF.

189

BETWEEN BITES OF ICE CREAM, I ASKED HER QUESTIONS. I WAS THERE TO INTERVIEW HER FOR A BEAUTY FEATURE. HER ANSWERS WERE BIZARRE.

SO, WHAT'S YOUR BIGGEST BEAUTY SECRET?

SERENITY.

TAPE RECORDER

OK, UM, WHAT'S ONE BEAUTY PRODUCT YOU NEVER LEAVE THE HOUSE WITHOUT?

MY HIGHER POWER.

IS THAT A SPECIFIC BRAND? BECAUSE WE NEED TO BE ABLE TO CALL THESE ITEMS IN AND SHOOT THEM.

OK, SO WHAT WOULD BE YOUR GO-TO BEAUTY TIP?

GO TO REHAB FOR DEPRESSION.

SHUFFLE SHUFFLE

SHE ENDED UP TELLING ME THE STORY OF HOW SHE'D VISITED HER SISTER AT A REHAB CENTER IN TEXAS, WHERE SHE WAS BEING TREATED FOR OVEREATING, AND WOUND UP CHECKING HERSELF IN, FOR DEPRESSION, ANGER, AND ISSUES OF CODEPENDENCE.

YOU WENT TO **REHAB** FOR DEPRESSION?

I DID, AND IT CHANGED MY LIFE. NOW, MY WORST DAY IS BETTER THAN MY BEST DAY BEFORE REHAB.

BUT HOW COULD YOU POSSIBLY GET DEPRESSED, LIVING THIS LIFE?

SHE TOLD ME ABOUT HER UPBRINGING, WHICH SOUNDED POSITIVELY GOTHIC: THIRTEEN DIFFERENT SCHOOLS IN TWELVE YEARS. ABUSE. ALCOHOLISM. CONSTANT MOVING AROUND. MY OWN UPBRINGING, BY COMPARISON, SEEMED LIKE **FATHER KNOWS BEST.**

SHE'D UNKNOWINGLY PLANTED A SEED.

191

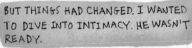

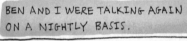

I'M PULLING INTO IN-N-OUT BURGER....HANG ON.

BUT THINGS HAD CHANGED. I WANTED TO DIVE INTO INTIMACY. HE WASN'T READY.

I WANT TO COME TO L.A. FOR YOUR BIRTHDAY.

I DON'T KNOW IF THAT'S A GOOD IDEA.

I BOOKED A TICKET ANYWAY.

I THOUGHT WE DISCUSSED THIS.

IF WE'RE GOING TO BE IN A RELATIONSHIP, THEN WE NEED TO BE IN A RELATIONSHIP. I'M SICK OF THIS LONG-DISTANCE BULLSHIT.

BUT WHEN I WENT TO L.A., I MET A DIFFERENT BEN.

SO THEN I TOLD SYLVIE... BEN—ARE YOU LISTENING?

YEAH, BABE, I JUST HAVE TO CHECK MY E-MAILS BECAUSE I'M WAITING FOR A MESSAGE FROM MY MANAGER.

HANG ON. I'VE GOT TO READ THIS. WHAT THE FUCK? THIS IS REDONKULOUS!

REDONKULOUS?!

THE VISIT WAS NEARLY UNBEARABLE.

WHAT DO YOU THINK A HEART ATTACK FEELS LIKE?

I DON'T KNOW...

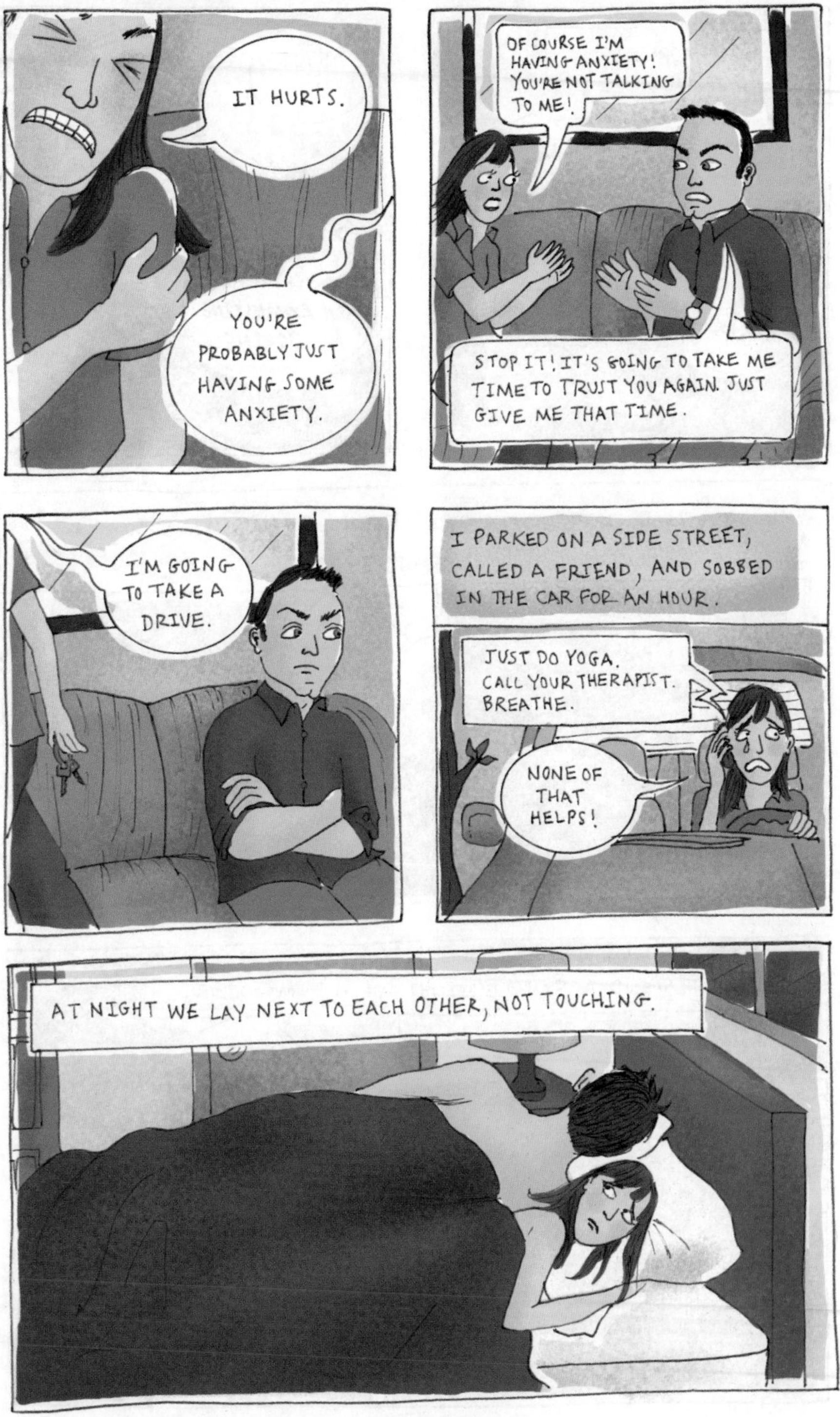
IT HURTS.
YOU'RE PROBABLY JUST HAVING SOME ANXIETY.
OF COURSE I'M HAVING ANXIETY! YOU'RE NOT TALKING TO ME!
STOP IT! IT'S GOING TO TAKE ME TIME TO TRUST YOU AGAIN. JUST GIVE ME THAT TIME.
I'M GOING TO TAKE A DRIVE.
I PARKED ON A SIDE STREET, CALLED A FRIEND, AND SOBBED IN THE CAR FOR AN HOUR.
JUST DO YOGA. CALL YOUR THERAPIST. BREATHE.
NONE OF THAT HELPS!
AT NIGHT WE LAY NEXT TO EACH OTHER, NOT TOUCHING.

THE NEXT MORNING . . .

CAN WE TALK?

ABOUT WHAT?

ABOUT US.

THESE CONVERSATIONS ARE *EXHAUSTING* AND *BORING*.

THE ONLY TIME I FELT *SAFE* WAS AFTER I'D DRUNK A BOTTLE OF WINE AND POPPED A COUPLE OF AMBIEN.

I DIDN'T SPEND A SINGLE NIGHT WITH HIM SOBER.

ON MY LAST NIGHT IN L.A., WE WENT TO SEE A MOVIE. IT WAS A POOR CHOICE: THE MOVIE, ABOUT DAMAGED RELATIONSHIPS, SEEMED TO HIGHLIGHT EVERY ISSUE WE WERE HAVING.

I LOOKED AT THE PROFILE OF HIS FACE IN THE DARK: I HAD TO BREAK UP WITH HIM NOW! I COULDN'T WAIT ANOTHER MINUTE! THEN I TOOK A BREATH. NO, I WAS JUST PROJECTING. WHAT WAS BEING PLAYED OUT UP THERE HAD NOTHING TO DO WITH US.

I PUT MY HAND ON HIS ARM AND STROKED IT. HE DIDN'T MOVE. HE WAS IGNORING ME! I WAS BEING ABANDONED!

WHERE ARE YOU GOING?

TO THE BATHROOM.

I TOOK THREE DEEP BREATHS AND LOOKED AT MY REFLECTION.

CALM DOWN.

LATER THAT NIGHT...

I THINK I SHOULD MOVE TO L.A.

I'M NOT READY FOR THAT.

THIS CONFIRMS EVERYTHING I EVER SUSPECTED! YOU WERE CHASING ME BECAUSE YOU COULDN'T HAVE ME!

THAT'S BULLSHIT!

THAT NIGHT, WE WENT THROUGH THE MOTIONS OF "CUDDLING," BUT WE WERE EACH IN OUR OWN WORLD. (AND I WAS, LITERALLY.) THOSE EARLY WORDS OF BEN'S HAUNTED ME: "THE MOST LONELY I'VE EVER FELT WAS WHEN I WAS IN A RELATIONSHIP THAT WASN'T WORKING."

Blackout

I OPENED MY E-MAIL TO FIND A MESSAGE FROM ASHLEY.

HEY, GIRL, HOW ARE YOU?

MAYBE IT'S BECAUSE SHE'D CONFIDED IN ME OR BECAUSE I WAS ENAMORED WITH HER ASHLEY-JUDD-NESS, I DON'T KNOW, BUT I FOUND MYSELF TELLING HER EVERYTHING THAT HAD BEEN GOING ON IN MY LIFE.

I'M MISERABLE.... I'M FIGHTING WITH MY BOYFRIEND.... I THINK I MIGHT BE ADDICTED TO AMBIEN.

WHAT I DIDN'T TELL HER WAS THE EXTENT OF MY ADDICTION. FIVE MILLIGRAMS OF AMBIEN ONCE A WEEK ON SUNDAY NIGHTS HAD TURNED INTO FIFTEEN TO TWENTY MILLIGRAMS NIGHTLY.

THOUGH THE LABEL HAD WARNED NOT TO MIX IT WITH ALCOHOL, I DRANK FREELY. SOMETIMES I WASHED DOWN A PILL WITH A SIP OF RED WINE.

"SLEEP-EATING" WAS A KNOWN SIDE EFFECT OF AMBIEN: I HAD STARTED WAKING UP WITH PREPARED PLATES OF FOOD IN MY BED.

CHEESE. CRACKERS. KNIFE. (HEY, AT LEAST I WAS CLASSY.)

197

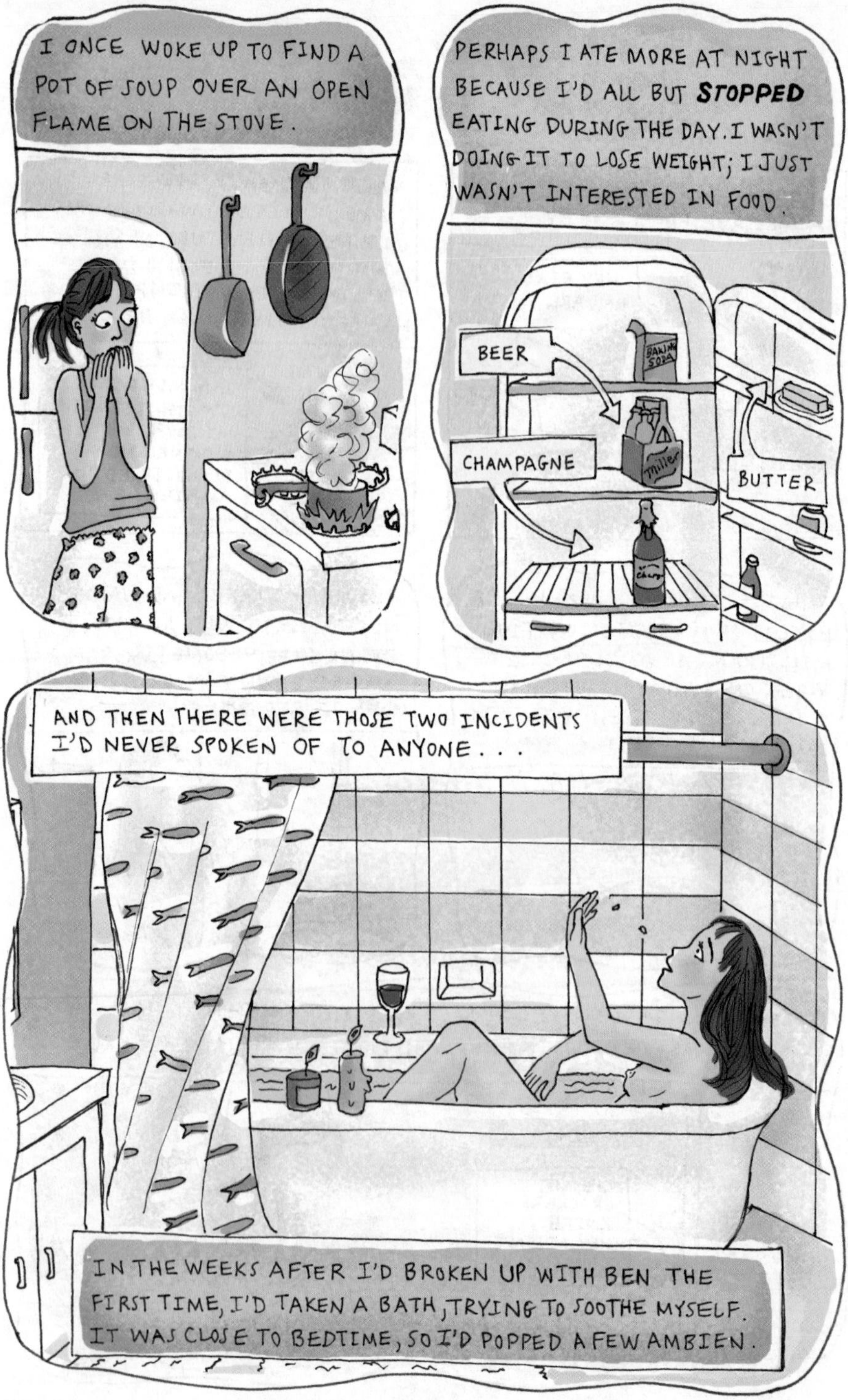
I ONCE WOKE UP TO FIND A POT OF SOUP OVER AN OPEN FLAME ON THE STOVE.
PERHAPS I ATE MORE AT NIGHT BECAUSE I'D ALL BUT **STOPPED** EATING DURING THE DAY. I WASN'T DOING IT TO LOSE WEIGHT; I JUST WASN'T INTERESTED IN FOOD.
BEER
BAKING SODA
Miller
CHAMPAGNE
BUTTER
AND THEN THERE WERE THOSE TWO INCIDENTS I'D NEVER SPOKEN OF TO ANYONE...
IN THE WEEKS AFTER I'D BROKEN UP WITH BEN THE FIRST TIME, I'D TAKEN A BATH, TRYING TO SOOTHE MYSELF. IT WAS CLOSE TO BEDTIME, SO I'D POPPED A FEW AMBIEN.

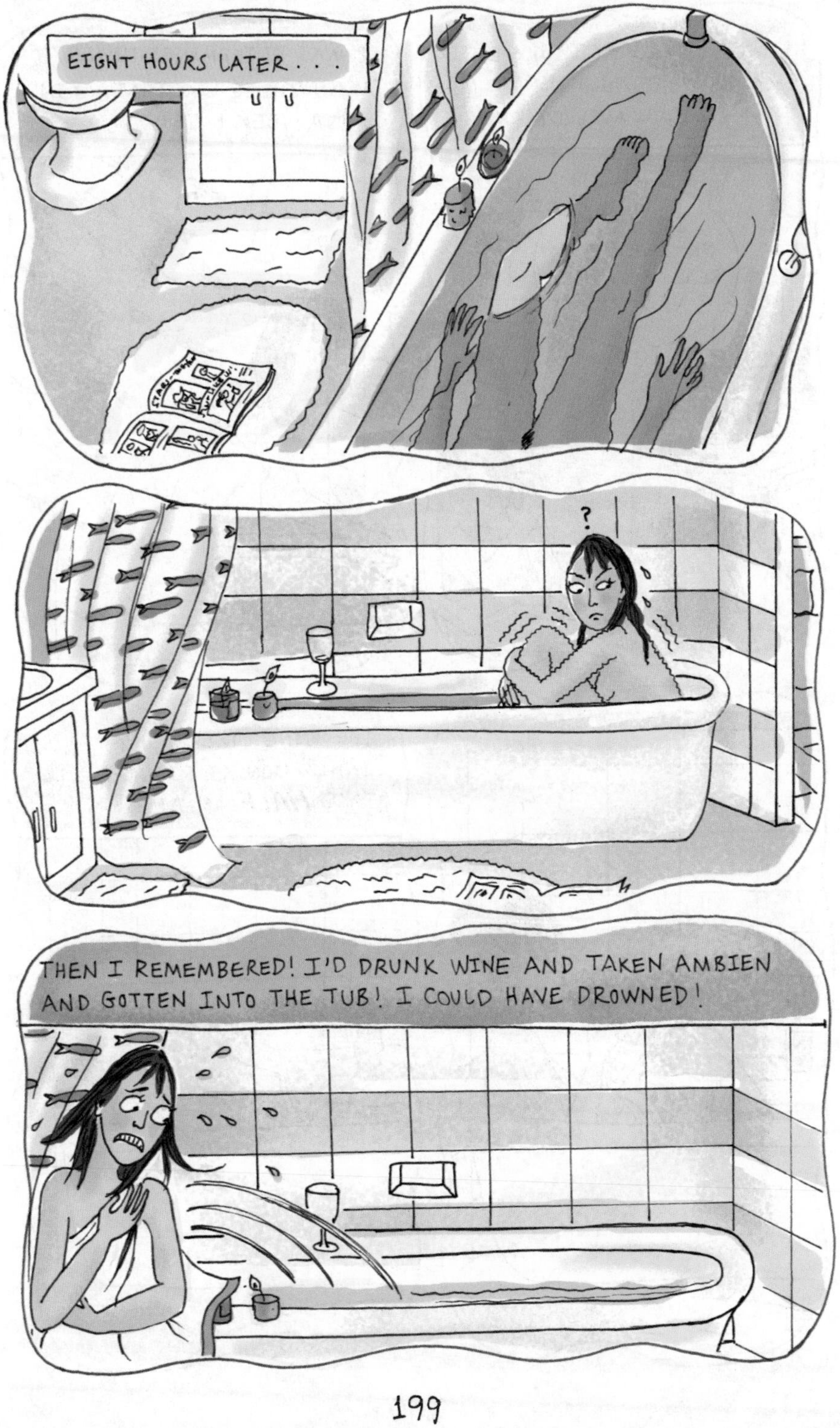
EIGHT HOURS LATER . . .
?
THEN I REMEMBERED! I'D DRUNK WINE AND TAKEN AMBIEN AND GOTTEN INTO THE TUB! I COULD HAVE DROWNED!

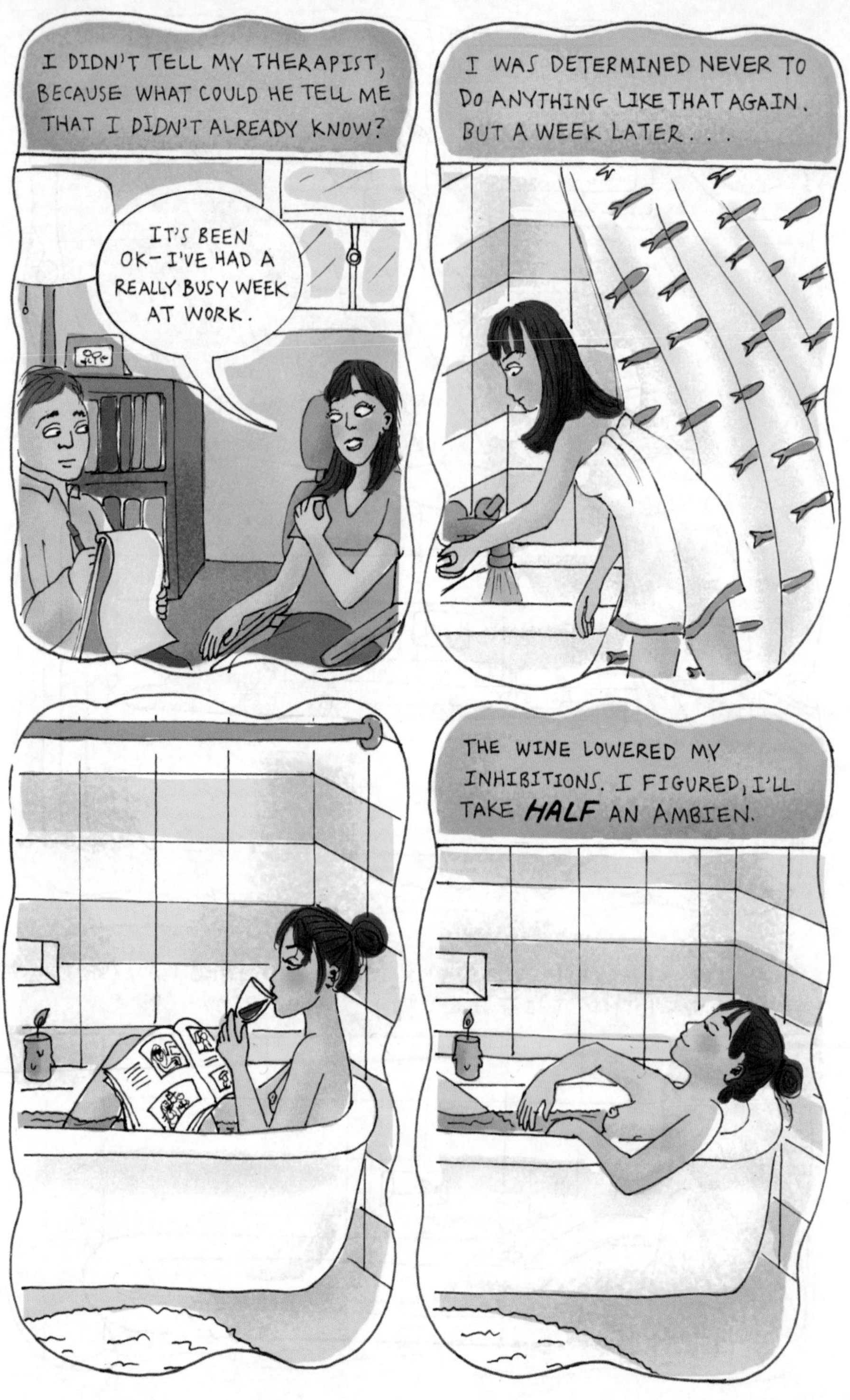
I DIDN'T TELL MY THERAPIST, BECAUSE WHAT COULD HE TELL ME THAT I DIDN'T ALREADY KNOW?
IT'S BEEN OK–I'VE HAD A REALLY BUSY WEEK AT WORK.
I WAS DETERMINED NEVER TO DO ANYTHING LIKE THAT AGAIN. BUT A WEEK LATER . . .
THE WINE LOWERED MY INHIBITIONS. I FIGURED, I'LL TAKE HALF AN AMBIEN.

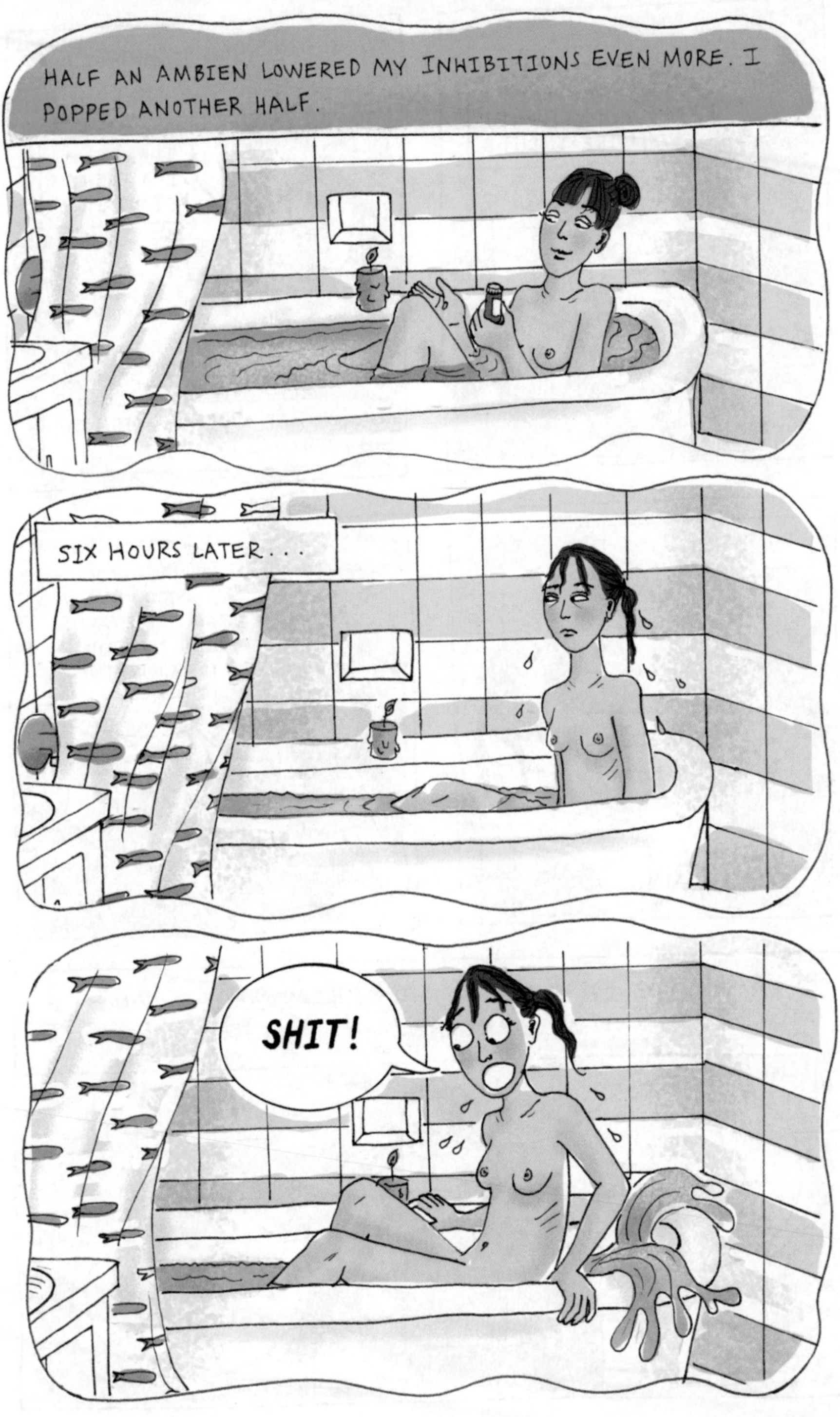
HALF AN AMBIEN LOWERED MY INHIBITIONS EVEN MORE. I POPPED ANOTHER HALF.
SIX HOURS LATER...
SHIT!

HAVE YOU EVER CONSIDERED IN-PATIENT TREATMENT?

SHE SENT ME A LINK TO THE PLACE SHE'D GONE: WWW.SHADESOFHOPE.COM

THANKS— I'LL THINK ABOUT IT.

I HAD NO INTENTION OF THINKING ABOUT IT.

BUT THEN . . .

ASHLEY JUDD SUGGESTED I CALL.... I CAN'T STOP TAKING AMBIEN. I'M DRINKING EVERY NIGHT OF THE WEEK.

WE SPOKE FOR FORTY-FIVE MINUTES. THE WOMAN ASKED ME ALL KINDS OF QUESTIONS, MANY OF WHICH DIDN'T SEEM TO APPLY.

MY ALCOHOL USE? NOT MUCH— TWO OR THREE GLASSES A DAY.

OF COURSE I DRINK ALONE: I'M SINGLE.

202

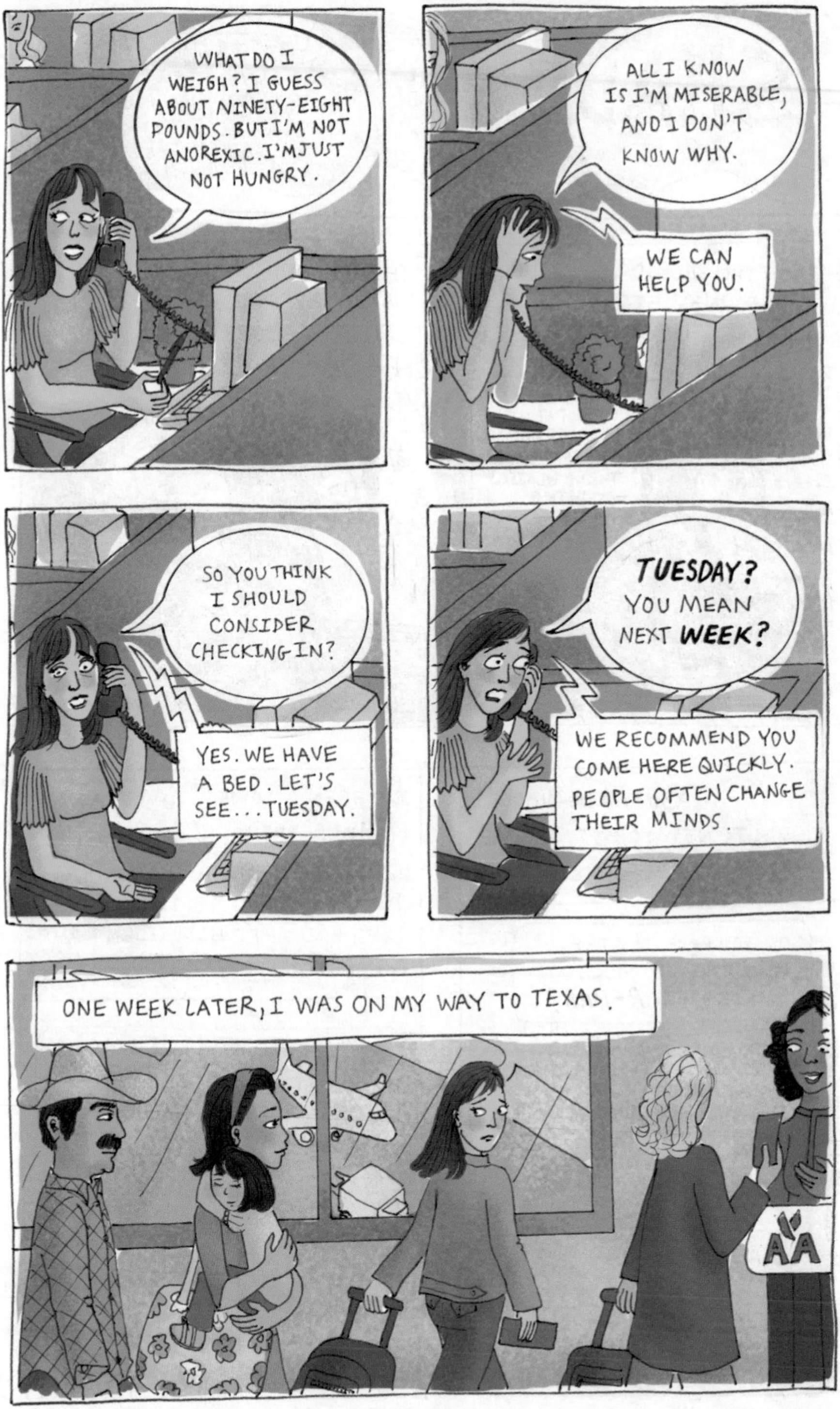
WHAT DO I WEIGH? I GUESS ABOUT NINETY-EIGHT POUNDS. BUT I'M NOT ANOREXIC. I'M JUST NOT HUNGRY.
ALL I KNOW IS I'M MISERABLE, AND I DON'T KNOW WHY.
WE CAN HELP YOU.
SO YOU THINK I SHOULD CONSIDER CHECKING-IN?
YES. WE HAVE A BED. LET'S SEE... TUESDAY.
TUESDAY? YOU MEAN NEXT WEEK?
WE RECOMMEND YOU COME HERE QUICKLY. PEOPLE OFTEN CHANGE THEIR MINDS.
ONE WEEK LATER, I WAS ON MY WAY TO TEXAS.
AA

SHADES OF HOPE

ON THE SECOND LEG OF THE TRIP THE PLANE HAD ONLY EIGHT SEATS, BUT I WASN'T AFRAID.

TOOK TWENTY MILLIGRAMS OF AMBIEN, DRANK THREE GLASSES OF WINE.

I THOUGHT ABOUT BEN, WHO'D FLOWN TO NEW YORK TO SEE ME THE WEEKEND BEFORE I'D LEFT.

OK, YOU PROBABLY TAKE A LITTLE TOO MUCH AMBIEN. BUT **REHAB?**

DO YOU KNOW HOW MANY TIMES I'VE TAKEN AMBIEN AROUND YOU? I WAS ON IT ALMOST EVERY TIME WE HAD SEX!

I'D BEEN ALLOWED TO GET AWAY WITH ANYTHING, BECAUSE BEN DIDN'T QUESTION A THING THAT I DID. FEAR OF LOSING MY LOVE HAD KEPT HIM SILENT AND COMPLIANT.

SOMETIMES YOU WERE A BIT OUT OF IT, BUT OUR SEX LIFE WAS GREAT.

I WASN'T THERE. EVER.

A WOMAN MET ME AT THE AIRPORT IN BUFFALO GAP. SHE COULD HAVE BEEN ONE OF MY SORORITY SISTERS.

WELL, **HI** THERE!

HI.

SHE CHATTERED ALL THE WAY TO SHADES OF HOPE. I WAS TOO OUT OF IT TO ASK HER WHAT TO EXPECT.

FIFTEEN MINUTES LATER, WE ARRIVED. IT DIDN'T LOOK LIKE THE TYPE OF PLACE ASHLEY JUDD WOULD REST HER HEAD.

THIS IS IT?

YEP, THIS IS HOME!

WE'LL GIVE YOU THIS BACK WHEN YOU CHECK OUT...AND THIS...AND THIS....

YEP, CELL PHONE, PRESCRIPTION MEDS, OH, AND THIS PURSE MIRROR — WE DON'T ALLOW ANYTHING WITH SHARP EDGES.

WAIT — MY IPOD?

ASHLEY HADN'T MENTIONED ANY OF THIS. WHERE WERE THE PRETTY OAK TREES? THE YOGA STUDIO?

I DIDN'T SEE THE SERENITY GARDEN.

OH, YOU WON'T SEE **THAT** FOR A WHILE. YOU'RE ON GENERAL MONITOR — SO YOU CAN'T LEAVE THE FRONT PORCH OF THE HOUSE.

WHAT'S GENERAL MONITOR?

SO MANY QUESTIONS! WAIT RIGHT HERE, AND I'LL BRING YOU DINNER.

I ALREADY ATE.

BETTER GET HUNGRY, THEN!

206

I ATE HALF OF THE DINNER SHE
SERVED AND PUSHED THE REST AWAY.

I DON'T
LIKE FISH.

WE DON'T DO
"HATE FOODS"
HERE.

POKE

POKE

POKE

LATER THAT NIGHT, I WAS SHOWN TO MY ROOM.

YOU'RE NOT
IN THE DORMS?
LUCKY!

207

MY ROOMMATES:

HI, I'M PAMELA.

PAMELA WAS FORTY-EIGHT AND AN ALCOHOLIC. IT WAS HER FIRST NIGHT THERE TOO.

RACHEL WAS A RAGEAHOLIC. HER HUSBAND HAD INSISTED SHE GET TREATMENT AFTER SHE THREW A LAMP AT HIS HEAD.

WHERE'S THE SPA IN THIS DUMP?!

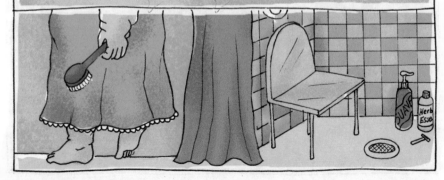

JANELLE, A COMPULSIVE OVEREATER, WEIGHED AT LEAST FOUR HUNDRED POUNDS. SHE NEEDED ASSISTANCE IN ORDER TO SHOWER.

208

I COULDN'T SEE HOW I FIT IN WITH THAT MOTLEY CREW. IN FACT, I WAS DETERMINED NOT TO.

SO WHAT'S YOUR POISON? ALCOHOL? PILLS? FOOD?

I DON'T KNOW.

AT 9:30 PM, WE LINED UP OUTSIDE THE NURSE'S OFFICE TO GET OUR MEDS. THE NURSE REFUSED TO GIVE ME AMBIEN.

BUT I'M SUPPOSED TO BE TAPERED OFF THE STUFF! I CAN'T JUST STOP COLD TURKEY!

THERE'S NO NOTE FROM MY SUPER-VISOR, SO I CAN'T GIVE IT TO YOU.

BUT I WON'T SLEEP A *WINK* TONIGHT!

I DIDN'T.

BY THE TIME TWO WEEKS HAD GONE BY, I'D SETTLED INTO A ROUTINE. IT WAS ALMOST IMPOSSIBLE NOT TO, SINCE EVERY DAY AT SHADES STARTED AT 6 AM AND WAS THE SAME.

"GENERAL MONITOR," IT TURNED OUT, MEANT I WAS CONFINED TO A SMALL AREA OF THE PREMISES.

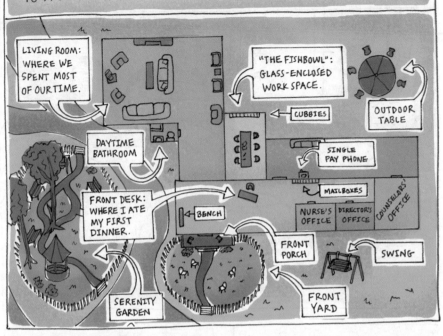

LIVING ROOM: WHERE WE SPENT MOST OF OUR TIME.

"THE FISHBOWL": GLASS-ENCLOSED WORK SPACE.

CUBBIES

OUTDOOR TABLE

DAYTIME BATHROOM

SINGLE PAY PHONE

MAILBOXES

NURSE'S OFFICE

DIRECTOR'S OFFICE

COUNSELORS' OFFICE

FRONT DESK: WHERE I ATE MY FIRST DINNER.

BENCH

FRONT PORCH

SWING

SERENITY GARDEN

FRONT YARD

I WAS ALSO ON "TABLE MONITOR"— I HAD TO EAT WITH TECHS, PEOPLE HIRED TO WATCH US.

AND "BATHROOM MONITOR," WHICH MEANT I HAD TO COUNT OUT LOUD WHILE ON THE TOILET, SO COUNSELORS COULD BE CERTAIN I WASN'T THROWING UP.

ONE... TWO... THREE...

I CAN'T HEAR YOU!

MOST OF OUR DAY WAS SPENT IN A SINGLE ROOM.

THE CLOSE QUARTERS CREATED FRICTION.

LISA, MICHELLE WON'T STOP STARING AT ME!

WHICH, I LATER LEARNED, WAS EXACTLY WHAT THE COUNSELORS WANTED.

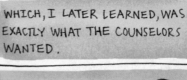

TAKE IT TO GROUP.

THE PLACE WAS **NOTHING** LIKE WHAT I EXPECTED.

ON-SITE MASSEUSE

TOKEN CELEBRITY

THINK THINK THINK

HOT GUY TO MAKE OUT WITH.

DARE TO B
DIFFER

AT THE SAME TIME, THE RIGOROUS ROUTINE AND STRICT RULES WERE GOOD FOR ME. I WAS LEARNING TO SURRENDER BECAUSE I HAD NO CHOICE.

I KNOW I DRINK **OFTEN**, BUT I DON'T DRINK **A LOT**.

ALL IT TAKES IS THAT FIRST DRINK. NO ONE EVER GOT RUN OVER BY A TRAIN'S CABOOSE.

INSTEAD OF ACTING OUT ON OUR ADDICTIONS, WE WROTE. I WROTE A HISTORY OF MY AMBIEN ABUSE, A HISTORY OF MY LOVE ADDICTIONS, A LIST OF MY FATHER'S TRANSGRESSIONS, DETAILS ABOUT MY SEX LIFE. . . . *EVERYTHING.*

I QUICKLY BECAME THE DOSTO-YEVSKY OF RECOVERY, DEDICATING HUNDREDS OF PAGES TO MY ISSUES. (I HAD SO MANY OF THEM, AFTER ALL.)

OW.

THE REST OF MY TIME WAS SPENT IN GROUP THERAPY.

LET LIVE

NAMES, CLAIMS, AND FEELINGS?

THOSE AREN'T *FEELINGS,* PEOPLE!

BORED.

ITCHY.

FULL.

214

ONCE A WEEK, THEY BUSSED US TO OUTSIDE AA MEETINGS.

S'THIS WEEKEND, I GEARED UP MY TRUCK AND TOOK HER TO DALLAS.

I FELT ALMOST HUMAN IN THOSE MEETINGS, LISTENING TO PEOPLE TALK ABOUT THEIR LIVES.

SOON, I BEGAN TO SEE TINY, BUT NOTICEABLE CHANGES TAKING PLACE IN MYSELF.

OOH, PAMELA, THIS ONE IS FOR YOU. "'NO' IS A COMPLETE SENTENCE."

GOOD ONE.

AT TIMES WE HAD BREAKOUT, UNEXPECTED FUN.

TEN SPLENDA PACKETS!

ON THE TWELFTH DAY OF *REEEHAB*, MY TRUE LOVE GAVE TO ME...

TWELVE CONFRONTATIONS!

ELEVEN COUNSELORS YELLING!

EVERY SATURDAY, WE HAD AN OUTING OF OUR OWN CHOOSING.

BEAUTY SCHOOL

BEAD STORE

MINI-GOLF

UNLESS SOMEONE RUINED IT FOR THE WHOLE GROUP.

TINA, YOU'RE LATE. I DON'T SEE A SATURDAY RECOVERY MOVIE IN THIS GROUP'S FUTURE.

BUT WE'RE SUPPOSED TO SEE **28 DAYS**!

I STARTED TO EXPERIMENT WITH PRAYER.

DIE-HARD, LIFELONG ATHEIST

THEN, A MONTH INTO TREATMENT . . .

BUT I'M JEWISH!

SO AM I.

OK, IT DIDN'T EXACTLY HAPPEN LIKE THAT. BUT AFTER A WHILE, I **DID** START TO FEEL A SPIRITUAL CONNECTION TO SOMETHING — NATURE, A HIGHER POWER, CALL IT WHAT YOU WILL. IT WAS SOMETHING GREATER THAN MY FATHER AND GREATER THAN ME.

I DIDN'T FEEL ANXIOUS; I WASN'T OBSESSING ABOUT BEN; AND I WAS SLEEPING SOUNDLY WITHOUT DRUGS FOR THE FIRST TIME IN A DECADE.

IN GROUP THERAPY SESSIONS, THE COUNSELORS STARTED PUSHING ME TO BREAK UP WITH BEN.

YOU'VE SAID YOU FEEL AMBIVALENT ABOUT HIM AND THAT HE DOESN'T SUPPORT YOU IN YOUR RECOVERY.

I SAID HE DOESN'T THINK I NEED IT.

THEY EVEN SUGGESTED I THROW OUT MY TABLOIDS.

MUST I GIVE UP **EVERYTHING** THAT MEANS **ANYTHING** TO ME?

IT'S ANOTHER WAY TO AVOID DEALING WITH YOUR FEELINGS.

218

EACH WEEK, WE WERE ALLOWED TWO SUPERVISED PHONE CALLS. I CALLED BEN ON THE SLY — I DIDN'T WANT ANYONE LISTENING IN ON US.

IT'S LIKE BOOT CAMP HERE!

OH MY GOD. I WOULDN'T SURVIVE ONE MINUTE. I MISS YOU.

I MISSED HIM TOO. BEN WAS THE FIRST PERSON I'D EVER KNOWN WHO'D LOVED ME UNCONDITIONALLY.

I'LL BE FLYING TO THE EAST COAST ON THURSDAY. I WISH THAT I COULD PARACHUTE INTO YOUR BED.

AND YET, THERE WERE CERTAIN THINGS I COULDN'T TALK TO HIM ABOUT.

IT'S COOL, THOUGH. I'M LEARNING ABOUT SOME INTERESTING THINGS LIKE, UM, GOD.

GOD?!

I COULDN'T HELP BUT THINK ABOUT SOMETHING HE'D SAID IN A TENDER MOMENT WE'D HAD, THE WEEKEND BEFORE I'D LEFT FOR SHADES.

I'M AFRAID YOU'RE GOING TO GROW SO MUCH, YOU'RE NOT GOING TO WANT TO BE WITH ME ANYMORE.

EVEN THEN, I'D SUSPECTED HE WAS RIGHT.

FAMILY WEEK

SHADES OF HOPE
TREATMENT CENTER

Panel 1:

I HAVE A SURPRISE FOR YOU. YOUR FAMILY IS COMING FOR FAMILY WEEK. YEP— EVEN YOUR DAD.

YOU'RE KIDDING.

ONLY MY SISTER KARYN COULDN'T COME. SHE HAD YEAR-OLD TRIPLETS.

Panel 2:

DURING FAMILY WEEK, RELATIVES WERE INVITED TO BUFFALO GAP TO PARTICIPATE IN THEIR LOVED ONE'S TREATMENT.

Panel 3:

OR, ON OCCASION, IN THEIR NEMESIS'S TREATMENT.

WHAT'S WRONG?

DO YOU THINK I WANT TO BE HERE?

Panel 4:

THAT AFTERNOON, WE MET FOR GROUP LECTURES ON CODEPENDENCE AND ALCOHOLISM. FAMILY MEMBERS WERE INSTRUCTED TO SIT SEPARATELY.

BUT IF I SAY NO, MY FAMILY MAKES ME FEEL GUILTY.

NO ONE CAN MAKE YOU FEEL ANYTHING WITHOUT YOUR CONSENT.

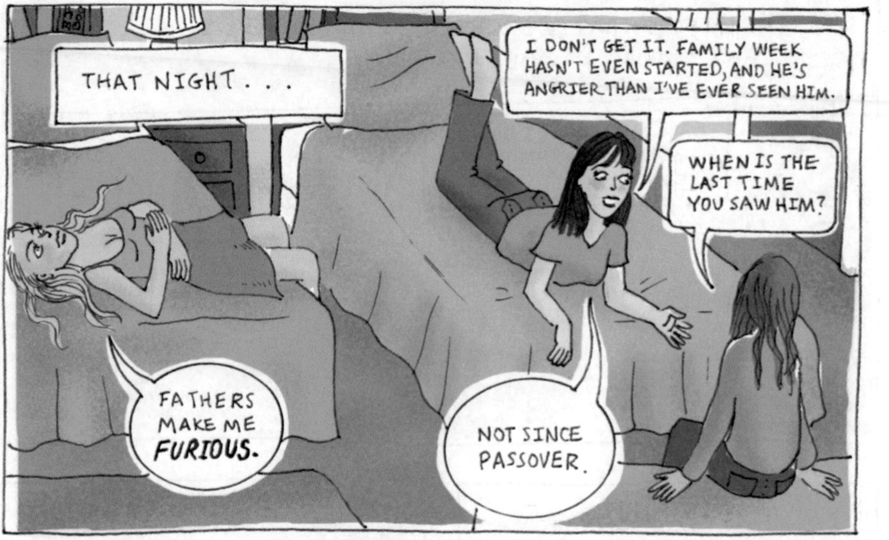
THAT NIGHT . . .
I DON'T GET IT. FAMILY WEEK HASN'T EVEN STARTED, AND HE'S ANGRIER THAN I'VE EVER SEEN HIM.
WHEN IS THE LAST TIME YOU SAW HIM?
FATHERS MAKE ME **FURIOUS.**
NOT SINCE PASSOVER.

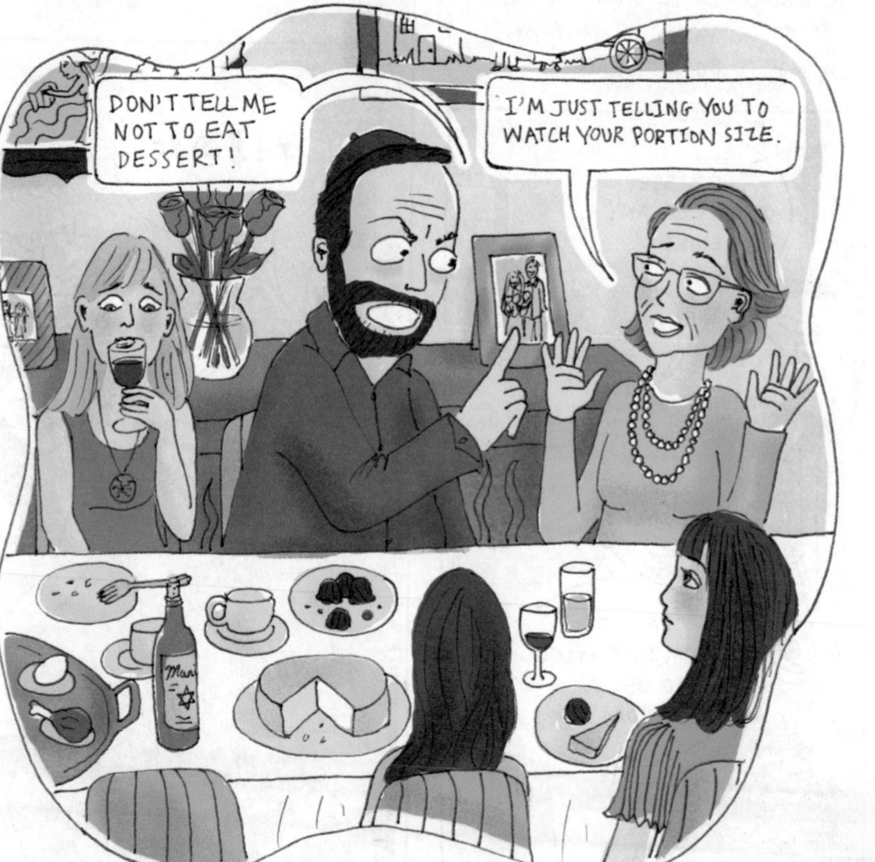
DON'T TELL ME NOT TO EAT DESSERT!
I'M JUST TELLING YOU TO WATCH YOUR PORTION SIZE.

THE TIME BEFORE THAT, WE'D BEEN GATHERED IN A HOSPITAL ROOM JUST BEFORE KARYN GAVE BIRTH.

LEAVE ME ALONE! I DON'T HAVE TO SIT IN THIS ROOM EVERY SECOND.

BILL...

IT OCCURRED TO ME THAT MY FATHER WAS PERPETUALLY FURIOUS, AND IT MIGHT NOT HAVE ANY- THING TO DO WITH ME.

THE BABIES COULD COME ANY SECOND!

DAMMIT, I'M JUST GOING TO GET A SODA!

NOR WAS IT MY JOB TO FIX IT.

*!$@#

ON THE SECOND DAY OF FAMILY WEEK, WE HAD READINGS. I SHARED EVERY SINGLE PIECE OF WRITING I'D DONE AT SHADES.

I HAD LITTLE TROUBLE EXECUTING JEREMY'S BIZARRE AND OFTEN UPSETTING REQUESTS, BUT THEN, I'D BEEN PRACTICING S AND M ALL MY LIFE. ONE MINUTE MY FATHER WAS SHOWERING ME WITH LOVE, THE NEXT HE WAS SCREAMING AT ME. IN A WAY, JEREMY AND I WERE A PERFECT FIT.

FINALLY, I WAS PURGING MY SECRETS, IN FRONT OF THE MAN WHO REFUSED TO GIVE UP HIS.

THEN I SPOKE TO WALTER MATHESON — IT TURNED OUT DAD HAD MET HIM AT A MALL AND ASKED FOR THIRTEEN THOUSAND DOLLARS.

WHEN I FINISHED, MY FAMILY WAS ALLOWED TO GIVE FEEDBACK.

NO ANALYSIS, CRITICISM, OR JUDGMENT — JUST "I SAW, I HEARD, I FELT."

IT'S OUTRAGEOUS... TO HAVE TO LISTEN TO THIS — THIS —

BUT IS IT *TRUE?*

YES.

MOM, DO YOU WANT TO GO NEXT?

I HEARD THAT WHEN SHE WAS YOUNG, SHE DIDN'T FEEL I PROTECTED HER. I FELT... PAIN.

FOR THE FIRST TIME, I SAW REAL FEAR ON MY FATHER'S FACE. AND MY MOTHER WASN'T RUSHING TO MAKE IT BETTER.

SO, WHAT — ARE YOU GOING TO LEAVE ME?

FOR AS LONG AS I COULD REMEMBER, I'D BEEN BEGGING HER TO LEAVE HIM — AND HAD BEEN EQUALLY TERRIFIED THAT SHE MIGHT GO THROUGH WITH IT.

HI, DAD. DO YOU NEED SOME MONEY?

TV DINNER

MILK CRATE

IF SHE LEFT HIM, WHERE WOULD THAT LEAVE ME?

THE QUESTION WENT UNANSWERED. THE DAY WAS OVER.

225

DAY THREE WAS AN EXPERIENTIAL FORM OF THERAPY CALLED A FAMILY SCULPT, DESIGNED TO SHOW A PHYSICAL MANIFESTATION OF THE FAMILY DYNAMIC. EACH OF US WERE ALLOWED TO "ARRANGE" OUR IMMEDIATE FAMILIES AS WE SAW THEM.

DAY FOUR WAS FOR GIVING AND RECEIVING CONFRONTATIONS— BASICALLY A HIGHLY STRUCTURED WAY TO SAY, "FUCK YOU."

THE ONLY APPROPRIATE RESPONSE TO A CONFRONTATION IS "THANK YOU."

FIRST, MY FATHER GAVE ME HIS.

THANK YOU.

WHEN YOU TOLD THE FAMILY ABOUT MY DEGREES, I THINK YOU BETRAYED ME, AND I FELT *EXTREME* RAGE.

I CONFRONTED HIM ABOUT TAKING OUT CREDIT CARDS IN MY NAME, RAGING AT ME, AND HIS NUMEROUS LIES. IT FELT GOOD TO SAY THOSE THINGS ALOUD AND TO HAVE THEM VALIDATED — IF BEGRUDGINGLY.

THANK YOU.

THE LAST DAY OF FAMILY WEEK WAS RESERVED FOR "LOVES, LIKES, AND FORGIVENESSES." WHEN THE TIME CAME TO FORGIVE MY FATHER, I BASICALLY FAKED IT.

UM, I LOVE YOUR IMAGINATION... AND YOUR GRANDIOSI — GENEROSITY.

THEN IT WAS MY FATHER'S TURN TO READ TO ME.

I LOVE YOUR OUTSIZED TALENT...YOUR SPIRIT... THE FACT THAT YOUR FRIENDS LOVE YOU SO MUCH.

PERHAPS HE'D HAD A CHANGE OF HEART BECAUSE HE WAS ABOUT TO BE EMANCIPATED?

OR MAYBE IT WAS JUST A SHOW. OVER HIS SHOULDER, I GLIMPSED THE FACES SURROUNDING US; THEY WERE SHINY WITH EMOTION.

EVERYONE IN THE **ROOM** WAS CRYING. I WANTED TO FEEL LIKE THEY DID, BUT I COULDN'T. AFTER YEARS OF LEARNING HOW NOT TO BELIEVE MY FATHER, I'D SUCCEEDED.

DID I PLAN TO LIVE THE REST OF MY LIFE AS A BITTER, ANGRY WOMAN-CHILD, PERPETUALLY SEEKING ANSWERS FOR THE CRIMES OF MY CHILDHOOD, OR WAS I GOING TO LET IT GO?

I WANTED TO LET IT GO. I **NEEDED** TO LET IT GO. IN THAT MOMENT, THAT MEANT TAKING MY FATHER'S RESPONSE AT FACE VALUE.

IT MEANT ACCEPTING HIM FOR WHO HE WAS, THEN AND NOW. IT MEANT REALIZING IT DIDN'T MATTER WHAT HIS MOTIVATIONS WERE, AS LONG AS I DIDN'T ALLOW HIM TO CONTINUE TO HURT ME.

PRETENDING ACTUALLY WORKED.

MY FAMILY HAD AN EARLY FLIGHT TO CATCH, SO AN HOUR LATER, WE WERE SAYING OUR GOOD-BYES.

THANK YOU FOR COMING. I KNOW YOU DIDN'T WANT TO.

I LOVE YOU, DARLING. I'M SORRY. I LOVE YOU.

AS I WATCHED THEM DRIVE AWAY, I PICTURED WHAT LIFE WOULD BE LIKE WHEN I GOT OUT. MY MOTHER WOULD GO TO RECOVERY MEETINGS FOR CODEPENDENCE. MY FATHER AND I WOULD SETTLE INTO A NEW KIND OF RELATIONSHIP— ONE WE'D BE FORGING FROM SCRATCH. MY SISTERS AND I WOULD RELATE TO EACH OTHER AS REAL ADULTS. MAYBE WE'D EVEN TALK ABOUT MUNDANE THINGS LIKE THE WEATHER.

I HOPED, I HOPED.

DECEMBER 24, 2006

NEVER HAD I BEEN SO HAPPY TO SEE MY APARTMENT. IT WAS CLEAN, LOVELY, AND MUCH BIGGER THAN I REMEMBERED.

SYLVIE AND MY MOTHER HAD CLEANED OUT MY LIQUOR CABINET, FLUSHED MY LAST BOTTLE OF AMBIEN, AND HAD EVEN TOSSED MY BELOVED TABLOID COLLECTION.

I CALLED BEN. HEARING HIS VOICE WAS BOTH COMFORTING AND STRANGELY DISTURBING.

HEYYY, WELCOME HOME.

WE CHATTED FOR A FEW AWKWARD MINUTES. I'D REFUSED TO BREAK UP WITH BEN IN TREATMENT. I WANTED TO SEE HIM AGAIN, THROUGH SOBER EYES.

THE MOVIE IS GOING WELL. IT LOOKS LIKE WE'RE GOING TO SCREEN IT FOR EXECS ON THE SIXTEENTH. HOW ARE YOU?

I'M REALLY GREAT. THANKS FOR ASKING.

I WOKE UP CHRISTMAS MORNING TO A WORLD THAT FELT MIRACULOUS.

EVERYTHING I DID THAT DAY, FROM RIDING THE SUBWAY, TO CALLING FRIENDS, TO COOKING MY OWN DINNER, FELT LIKE A GIFT.

IT WAS A FEELING I KNEW WOULDN'T LAST. BUT I WANTED TO HOLD ON TO IT FOR AS LONG AS I POSSIBLY COULD.

OVER THE NEXT FEW WEEKS, BEN AND I GOT TO KNOW EACH OTHER AGAIN. WE MAINTAINED A LIGHT, CAREFUL RAPPORT.

WHAT ARE YOU DOING TONIGHT?

I'M MAKING DINNER FOR GENEVIEVE AND TED: VEGETABLE LASAGNA AND SALAD. I LOVE TO COOK NOW!

AND WHILE IT WAS COMFORTING TO HEAR HIS VOICE, I COULDN'T LET HIM IN ON THE CHANGES I WAS GOING THROUGH.

IT WAS A PROCESS I WAS STILL STRUGGLING WITH. I'D BEEN A LIFELONG, DEVOUT ATHEIST. RELIGIOUS-SPEAK HAD ALWAYS SOUNDED TO ME LIKE HUCKSTERISM.

WHAT AM I *DOING?*

BEN AND I HAD BONDED OVER OUR MUTUAL DISDAIN OF THE SUBJECT ON MANY OCCASIONS.

I'D LIKE TO THANK GOD...

YEAH, GOD WAS TOO BUSY INFLUENCING THAT CASTING DIRECTOR TO WORRY ABOUT THE TSUNAMI.

AND YET, UNDENIABLY, THE MORE I GOT DOWN ON MY KNEES, THE MORE I TALKED TO GOD IN THE SHOWER, THE MORE I SURRENDERED TO THE IDEA OF UNCONDITIONAL LOVE (BOYFRIEND OR NO BOYFRIEND, FATHER OR NO FATHER), THE MORE I ACCEPTED MY CIRCUMSTANCES EXACTLY AS THEY WERE...

THE MORE I FELT TAKEN CARE OF, IN A WAY I'D NEVER BEFORE EXPERIENCED. I DIDN'T KNOW WHERE IT WAS GOING, OR IF IT WOULD STICK: I WAS ALL TOO AWARE OF MY TENDENCY TO DIVE HEADFIRST INTO THE IDEA DU JOUR. BUT I WANTED TO TRY IT.

AFTER ALL, THERE'D BEEN SOME-THING STANDING IN THE WAY THE WHOLE TIME: A HIGHER POWER OF MY OWN MAKING.

IT WAS TIME TO GIVE THAT UP. AND I DIDN'T WANT BEN TO MOCK ME FOR THROWING MYSELF INTO RECOVERY.

MEETING IS DOWNSTAIRS AT 7:00 P.M.

OR TO DRAG ME BACKWARDS INTO SKEPTICISM, CYNICISM, AND DOUBT. SO I REMAINED SILENT AND DIDN'T LET HIM IN.

RUNNING OUT TO MEET UP WITH KARYN FOR DINNER. I'LL CALL YOU LATER.

THE BIG BOOK

BY THE TIME I FLEW TO L.A. AGAIN, THE GULF BETWEEN US HAD WIDENED. WE SAT AT DINNER MAKING SMALL TALK, BEN DRINKING WATER IN SOLIDARITY WITH ME. THE THINGS WE'D ALWAYS TALKED ABOUT TO COVER UP OUR PROBLEMS — BOOKS, MOVIES, CELEBRITIES, OUR FRIENDS — FAILED TO PROVIDE THEIR USUAL SMOKE SCREEN.

OH, AND DEB AND RYAN BROKE UP.

WOW, REALLY?

THE THINGS WE **NEVER** TALKED ABOUT — MY DISSATISFACTION WITH THE RELATIONSHIP, HIS AMBIVALENCE ABOUT CHILDREN, OUR INTIMACY FEARS — REMAINED BURIED.

YEAH, AND HE'S ALREADY DATING SOMEONE ELSE; THIS CUTE BLONDE GIRL.

THAT WAS FAST.

I FELT MY HEART BREAKING AS I LOOKED AT HIM ACROSS THE TABLE. HE WAS A GOOD GUY WHO LOVED ME, BUT IF I STAYED WITH HIM, I COULDN'T GROW. BY THE TIME THAT FIRST NIGHT WAS UP, I KNEW I HAD TO BREAK UP WITH HIM FOR GOOD.

237

IT TOOK ME A FEW DAYS TO WORK UP THE NERVE TO TELL HIM. AND I STILL DIDN'T DO IT VERY ELOQUENTLY.

LET'S JUST...NOT TALK FOR A WHILE.

WE ENDED EVERY BREAKUP CONVERSATION THIS WAY. I COULDN'T SAY THE WORDS "IT'S OVER," AND HE COULDN'T HEAR THEM.

GOOD-BYE FOR NOW.

FOR NOW.

BUT THIS TIME, IT REALLY WAS OVER.

THAT WAS THE LAST TIME I EVER SAW HIM.

238

THE GOOD LIFE

I WAS GOING TO YOGA AGAIN AND ATTENDING REGULAR RECOVERY MEETINGS. THE MAGAZINE I WORKED FOR OFFERED ME A CONTRACT, WHICH MEANT I WAS ABLE TO WORK FROM HOME. I'D GOTTEN A DOG, A LITTLE TEN-POUND RESCUE NAMED VIOLET. LIFE WAS GOOD.

INTERVIEWING CELEBRITIES WAS DIFFERENT. THE SUBJECT OF MY FATHER NEVER CAME UP, AND STILL I WAS ABLE TO DRAW THEM OUT.

EVERYTHING WAS DIFFERENT.

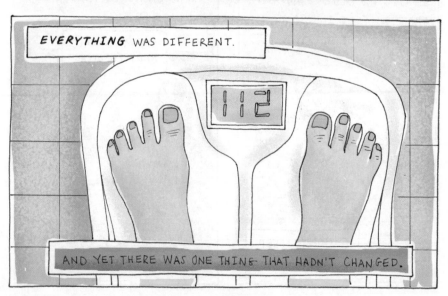

THANKSGIVING 2007

THE MINUTE I WALKED INTO MY AUNT'S CONDO, I SPOTTED MY FATHER. IT WAS HIS ISOLATION THAT MADE HIM SO NOTICEABLE.

LAURIE'S HERE!

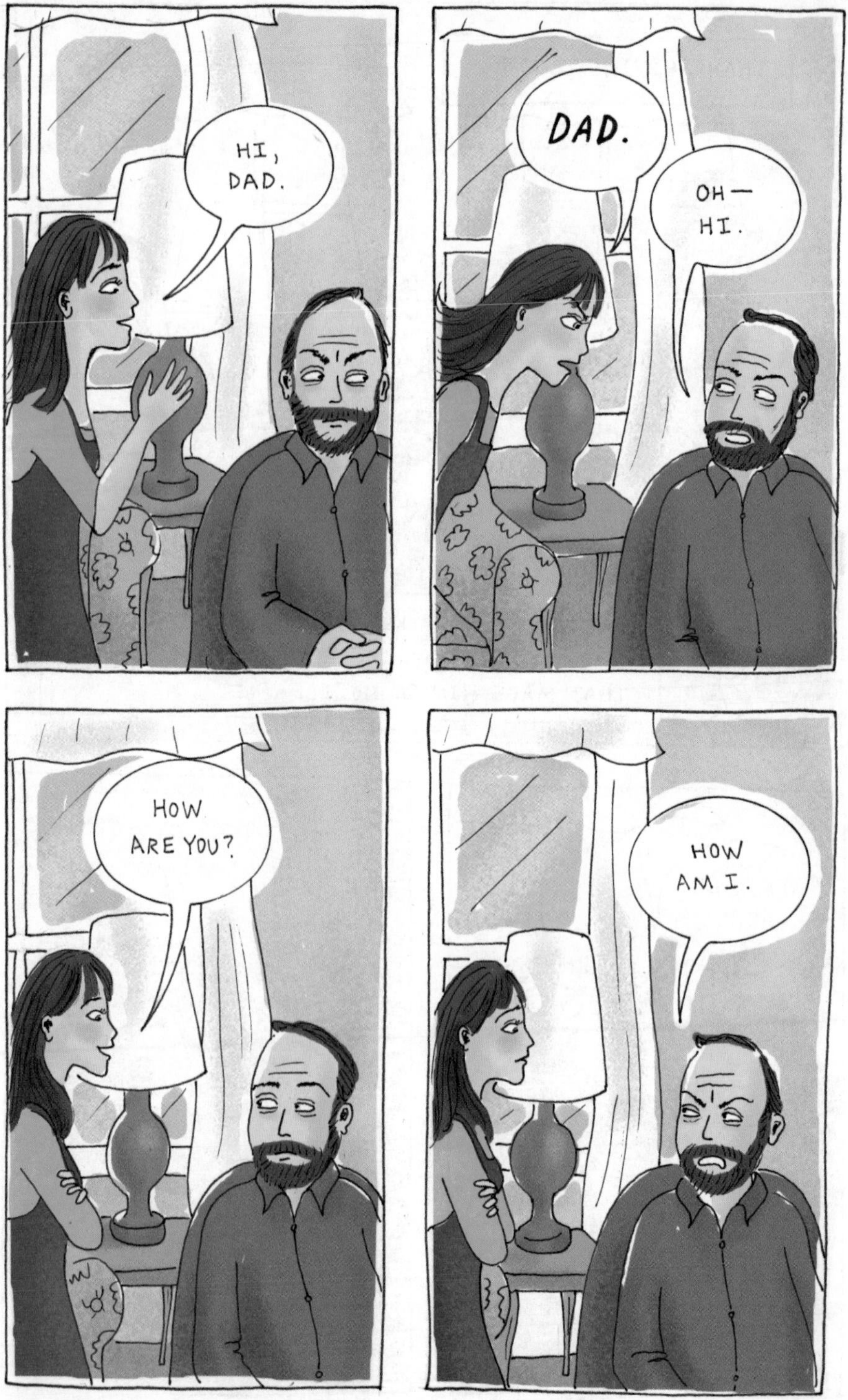
HI, DAD.
DAD.
OH— HI.
HOW ARE YOU?
HOW AM I.

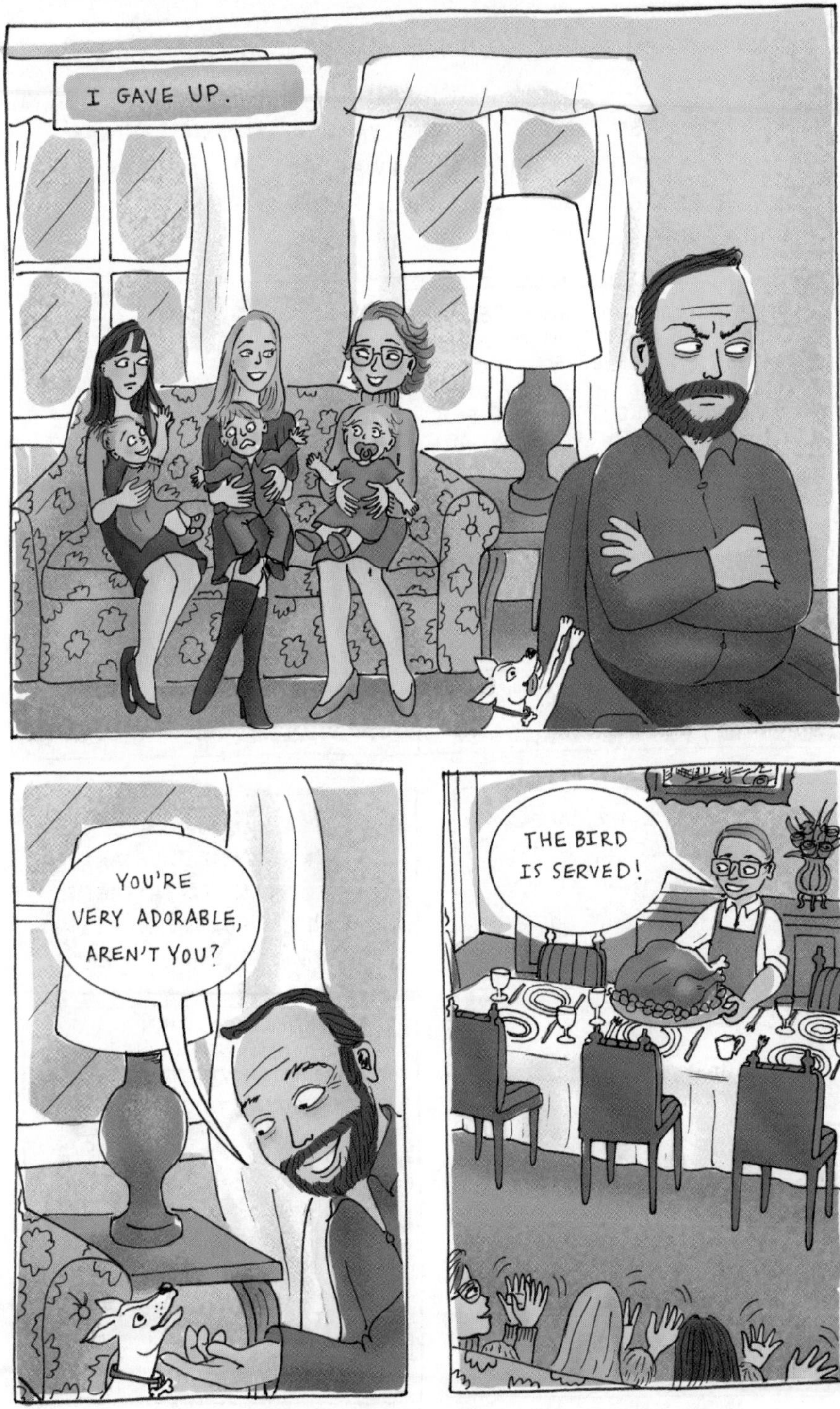
I GAVE UP.
YOU'RE VERY ADORABLE, AREN'T YOU?
THE BIRD IS SERVED!

I KNEW THEN I WAS NEVER GOING TO HAVE A FATHER
WHO WOULD ASK ME HOW I WAS DOING, LISTEN TO MY OPINIONS,
OR WORRY ABOUT MY EMOTIONAL WELL-BEING. HE'D NEVER
DONE ANY OF THOSE THINGS, ANYWAY, BUT I'D NEVER
LOST HOPE THAT HE MIGHT. ALL THAT WAS GOOD IN MY
FATHER WAS NOW CLOSED OFF TO ME TOO.

YOU SHOULD HAVE **SEEN** THE DINNERS AT MY AUNT'S HOUSE: EVERYBODY SCATTERED IN, AND THEY'D COOK FORTY CHICKENS, THREE OR FOUR ROASTS, THIRTY GALLONS OF SOUP, TWENTY PIES — THERE MUST HAVE BEEN ONE HUNDRED LOAVES OF BREAD — YOU ATE LIKE A HORSE! YOU SAT DOWN TO EAT AT ONE PM AND FINISHED AT FIVE IN THE AFTERNOON. IT WAS **WONDERFUL.**

NOR WOULD I EVER HAVE A
MOTHER WHO WOULD ATTEND
RECOVERY MEETINGS, AS I'D
IMAGINED SHE MIGHT ON THAT
LAST DAY AT SHADES.

VRRROOOM!

OR SISTERS WHO HAD ANY DESIRE
TO CONFRONT MY FATHER AND
FORCE A FAMILY TRUTH. THEY'D
LONG SINCE FORGIVEN HIS
TRANSGRESSIONS.

SOUNDS BETTER THAN
THE THANKSGIVING DINNERS
YOU HAD IN VIETNAM.

UGH, GROSS.

NONE OF THAT MATTERED ANYMORE. I KNEW WHAT I HAD TO DO.

CALL A BIT MORE OFTEN, OK?

IT HAD COST MY FAMILY TOO MUCH TO LIVE IN THEIR FICTIONS. I WASN'T WILLING TO PAY THE SAME PRICE.

NOVEMBER 22, 2007

Secrets

Whenever my father went out of town, he had the mail stopped.

EACH OF THE BRILLIANT PEOPLE PICTURED BELOW — FROM MY AGENT AT
AND HER TALENTED ASSISTANT, NATHAN ROSTRON, TO THE INCOMPARABLE
EDITED NUMEROUS EARLY DRAFTS AND LENT HER EXPERTISE
SUPPORTIVE FRIENDS — CONTRIBUTED TO THIS BOOK IN
WOULD NOT EXIST. (OK, IT MIGHT EXIST, BUT IT

MY HEARTFELT THANKS TO, FROM LEFT TO RIGHT (FIRST ROW): FIONA MAAZEL,
JESSIE WICK, NATHAN ENGLANDER, CAROLE RADZIWILL; (SECOND ROW)
NATHAN ROSTRON, MERRILL MARKOE, PAIGE POOLER, ASHLEY JUDD,
ROBERTSON, LESLIE ROBARGE, JILL HERZIG, MARYELLEN GORDON,
GELERNTER, DEREK LOOSVELT, MELISSA BELLINELLI; (FOURTH
BROWER, KRISTAN SAKS, STACEY PLATT, PATRICIA COLLINS, ABIGAIL
MARVIN, TANYA ASNES, ROBERT WILKINS. I ALSO THANK SHADES
THE CORPORATION OF YADDO, AND EDDIE STERN, RESPECTIVELY,
IN, AND TEACHING ME HOW TO BREATHE. I OWE A HUGE DEBT OF
TO MY MOTHER, FOR LOVING ME NO MATTER WHAT. FINALLY,
INSPIRED ME TO PICK UP THE PEN. I REMAIN IN AWE OF

246

ICM, AMANDA URBAN, TO MY EDITOR AT LITTLE, BROWN, JUDY CLAIN,
PAIGE POOLER, WHO DID THE COLOR, TO GENEVIEVE FIELD, WHO
THROUGHOUT EVERY STEP OF THE PROCESS, TO MY AMAZINGLY
ONE CRUCIAL WAY OR ANOTHER. WITHOUT THEM, THIS BOOK
WOULD BE A LOT LESS AWESOME.)

ANDY WARD, JENNY ROSENSTRACH, MY SISTERS KARYN AND SYLVIE,
JUDY CLAIN, AMANDA URBAN, GENEVIEVE FIELD, CINDI LEIVE,
AMANDA STERN; (THIRD ROW) AL MCEVOY, ARIEL FOXMAN, PAUL
ROB TOURTELOT, KAREN RAMOS, JOANNA BOBER, MELISSA
ROW) DANA CLORFENE, STEPH CORRADO, ALISSA QUART, ALISON
PESTA, TOM KEALEY, JENNIFER GISTRAK, KYLE SPENCER, CATE
OF HOPE TREATMENT CENTER, BLUE MOUNTAIN CENTER AND
FOR SAVING MY LIFE, GIVING ME BEAUTIFUL SPACES TO WORK
GRATITUDE TO "BEN," FOR HIS UNCONDITIONAL SUPPORT, AND
I WOULD LIKE TO ACKNOWLEDGE MY FATHER, WHO FIRST
HIS MYRIAD GIFTS.

247

About the Author

Laurie Sandell is a contributing editor at *Glamour*, where she writes cover stories, features, and personal essays. She has also written for *Esquire, GQ, New York,* and *InStyle*, among other publications. In her twenties, she spent four years traveling around the world, having unsavory experiences she later justified as "material."